Under the Lens

Literary Analysis of the Novel 'Outback Summer'

Dr. Robert R. Coenraads

Coenraads GEMS Publishing

First Published in Australia in 2025
by Coenraads GEMS Publishing, Sydney
www.robertcoenraads.com.au

Under the Lens. Literary Analysis of the Novel 'Outback Summer' by Robert Raymond Coenraads, 98 pp. 26,500 words, 6 x 9 in. (152.4 x 228.6 mm), Garamond 11.5 pt, line spacing 1.1, B&W on cream paper. Cover design, cover photo and illustrations by Robert Raymond Coenraads

A catalogue record for this book is available from the National Library of Australia

ISBN 978-1-923330-06-1

Outback Summer is available to enjoy in various formats
ISBN 978-1-923330-00-9 Paperback
ISBN 978-1-923330-01-6 Hardcover
ISBN 978-1-923330-02-3 Large print
ISBN 978-1-923330-03-0 E-book
ISBN 978-1-923330-04-7 Audiobook

DEDICATION

For my loved ones, so that they can know me better

CONTENTS

ACKNOWLEDGMENTS

I would like to thank Gerry Surha (Iljiddimor) for his cultural sensitivity review of my novel 'Outback Summer'

Congratulations Giddeelah (Black Cockatoo),

It was a pleasure to accompany Rod on his emotional, physical and spiritual journey as each chapter revealed itself to me. I was pleasantly surprised with the unexpected ending which I thought was a fitting climax to an unforgettable journey.

This book reflects so much content that I identify with as a First Nations' man growing up in my community and then venturing out into the big wide world.

As a First Nations' man, this novel took me back to a poignant time in my personal history and ignited memories of past experiences that I had lived through as a boy growing up in the 70's.

The emotional value of reading 'Outback Summer' for me was very high because it acknowledges and highlights the ignorance of a white Australia that existed in the 1970's and still today continues to fail, recognise and comprehend the struggle of First Nations peoples—our plea for equality in our own country.

Iljiddimoor (Sacred Rock)
Jiddabal/Mamu/Yidinji
Traditional Custodian

ACKNOWLEDGEMENTS

1. INTRODUCTON TO THE NOVEL *OUTBACK SUMMER*

Classification and Introduction

Outback Summer by Robert Coenraads is an award winning Australian coming-of-age 'bildungsroman' classified under the following headings:

- Books › Romance › Clean & Wholesome
- Books › Coming of Age Romance › Small Town Romance
- Books › Teen & Young Adult › Romance › Multicultural
- Books › Australiana

Under the guise of the young-adult romance genre, the author uses the romantic relationships of the naïve or unreliable protagonist, Rod Conway, a young man from the city, as a tool to explore and celebrate small-town Australian life in its full and rich diversity. *Outback Summer* explores sometimes-edgy, small-town, indigenous-colonial cultural relationships, the strong bond of 'mateship' within 'gang' groups, and the coming-of-age transition from youth to adulthood with the associated change in acceptable social settings and gathering places. The wholesome swimming pool, river, milk bar, bakery and cinema are superseded by more traditional adult gathering places, principally pubs and clubs where patrons become indoctrinated into the all-pervasive influences of pub and alcohol culture, and often suffer its negative consequences.

Language

Written in Australian English, the idiomatic language, slang and turn of phrase allow the reader a rare insight into Australia's iconic and unique outback town life and culture, where mateship remains king in the face of any adversity, be it drought, fire or flood.

For the benefit of the non-Australian reader, a glossary of terms is appended, many of which either had their humble beginnings in the outback, or were derived from a British colonial background, or were modified from First Nation languages.

Setting

The novel is set in the picturesque town of Bourke, 'Gateway to the Outback', in western New South Wales during the summers of 1978 and 1979. Although neither time nor place are relevant to the universal themes and issues explored in the novel, clues such as mention of the music, popular ABC TV programs, NSW school curriculum, car and motorcycle models, hotels and other businesses operating in Bourke reveal the era of the novel. The action takes place in the township and surrounding district, with placenames shown on the maps included in the front of the novel. Settings include wide-open desert spaces, mining camps, remote outback station homes on enormous landholdings, and the Darling River floodplain country, home to a variety of Australian wildlife.

Voice (Point of View)

The story is written in the third person and told from the protagonist's point of view with the action seen through the lens of his dialogue and restricted in its interpretation by his limited life experiences. Apart from minor excursions, the reader sits firmly perched on Rod Conway's shoulder throughout the story and therefore becomes invested emotionally in his widening and evolving point of view.

Storyline

Outback Summer opens as protagonist, Rod Conway, rides his motorcycle into the great dry Australian continental interior to work with his cousin René as field hand on a mineral exploration project—his first summer vacation job.

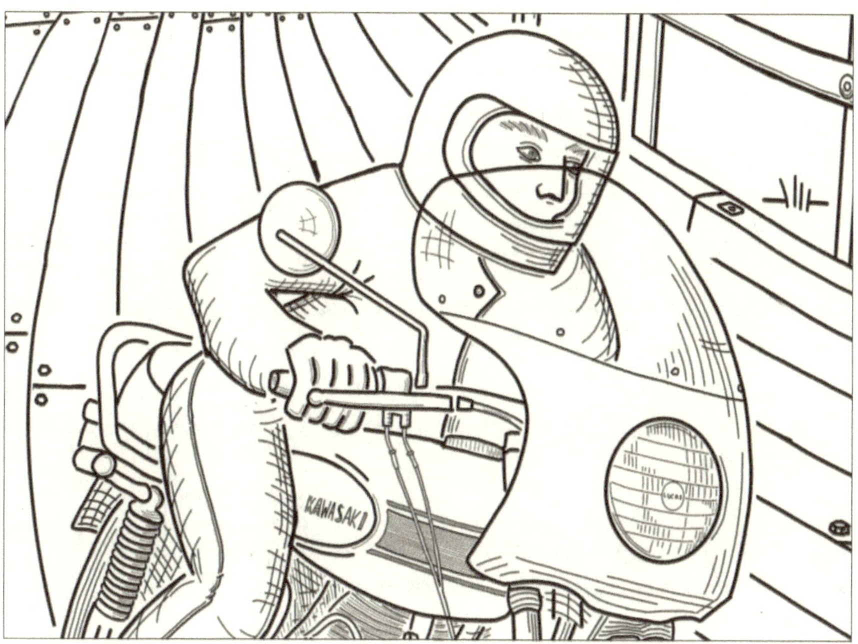

Rod, a 20-year-old university student, has lived a sheltered life in Sydney's leafy upper-class northern suburbs. He is intelligent, sensitive and willing to work hard, but is "empty headed' and naïve as far as the ways of the world—initially interested only in his studies and personal desires. As a result of living with his parents (who lovingly support his university studies), he sees everything from this egocentric viewpoint (as indeed do many teenagers from privileged backgrounds) and he must come to learn that others view their lives differently.

Being part of the rich, white, Australian elite of that time Rod has no understanding of issues faced by other socio-economic classes or racial groups such as poverty, discrimination, or even the need to struggle to establish oneself in a societal hierarchy. This is despite the fact that he is, himself, the son of Dutch immigrants who arrived in Australia in the 1950's. Rod's parents, believing it best for their children, immediately 'Australianised', switching to English as their first language, speaking it at home, anglicizing the names of their children and hiding any evidence of their own struggles from their children.

Rod's brain is a finely-honed instrument focused on hormone-fuelled ideas and emotions evolved over some 300,000 years since the appearance on anatomically-modern human race or indeed 2 billion years since the evolution of sexual reproduction in the animal kingdom. Sitting above this primitive evolutionary base is a clean slate with the capability to develop spiritually, philosophically and ideologically based on his experiences and observations of the world around him.

> *"Apart from studies and the usual hormone-fuelled turmoil of adolescence, there wasn't much going on inside his head—his mind a blank page waiting for life's experiences to imprint. Besides, there were more important things for a young bloke journeying into manhood to think about—like girls for one thing, and motorbikes for another."*

It is this process of growth that is explored by the author in the novel based on his own experiences in that time and place.

Everything about the town of Bourke is new and interesting to Rod, having never been away from his North Shore home, nor far from the caring but watchful eyes of his parents. Almost immediately as he distances himself from home's routine, he becomes more thoughtful and introspective, especially as new experiences and friendships cross the trajectory of his life's path.

Rod's easy-going nature means he is initially quickly accepted by the town's youth, forming easy friendships through work and socialising at the local swimming pool. But, as he settles in, Rod discovers that, despite being at a similar stage in life and on a similar journey to adulthood as his new friends, there are differences between them, rooted in their different upbringing, parental influences and expectations, educational level, socio-economic background, and even race.

In his quest for the important things of life—friendship and romance—Rod pushes all differences aside, bulldozing them out of his path and refusing to accept what he is discovering. 'People are people' and all are the same and equal' is the ideal he truly wants to believe.
Rod is initially unaware of the town's social norms as they are learned only through living a lifetime there, through a childhood of parental instructions, gestures, nuances and comments.

Dramatic Arc

The novel's plot follows a traditional five-part dramatic arc beginning with the exposition, or opening portion of the story, as described above. In chapters 1 and 2, the reader comes to know the protagonist, the setting and some of the other principal characters. This is followed by a slowly escalating dramatic tension. Rod is forced to piece together a complete picture of the town from what he discovers day by day, what people around him are telling him and how they are acting. Despite incident after incident in the story, Rod refuses to accept differences between people and doesn't fit into an expected behavioural norm.

> *But the implication of a difference between them—words like 'your people' or 'my people', 'your past' or 'my past'—made him sad. These evoked a sense of separation of him from her*

In Rod's mind, his outback summer expands into a lifetime, and he even refuses to accept the fact that he will eventually have to leave Bourke and return to his life in Sydney.

> *"Rod, you're gonna have to leave Bourke an' go back to Sydney at the end of summer, right?"*
> *She was far more pragmatic than Rod. She'd hit him with the very thought he'd pushed farthest from his mind; the horrible thought he was refusing to accept. He loved Bourke, his new friends and his work, and never wanted to leave the place. He knew his seemingly endless summer would eventually draw to a close and he would be duty-bound to return to Sydney, to the family home, to his university studies.*
> *"Yeah, I guess I will have to, Beth." He forced himself to say it, slowly; painfully.*

Rod constantly urges his new friends to strive for what they want to achieve in life—even though from his own viewpoint and experience he cannot grasp that his exhortations are far more difficult for them to achieve than they ever were for him. He urges them to choose what they want to achieve in life and not just be led to where generation after generation has gone before. However, his friends Ricky, Dan, Beth and Pete don't seem to have the same ambitions or mindset as his university friends back in Sydney.

As the story progresses Rod realises that the adult world to which his new friends are aspiring differs from his own. Such a world holds little of interest for him being likely to end in entrenched racism, alcohol abuse, even violence, but it is a destiny to which they seem to be drawn.

Tension arises from beginning of the novel through the ever-present menace of the shadowy character 'Dark Rider' and that threat continues to grow to the point where Rod is personally intimidated by him at the Oxford Hotel. Dark Rider turns out to be Dan's brother, Brad, who sees Rod as an outsider with no right to be part of the town's social groups, and a threat to their local girls—a thief of property that rightfully belongs to them. Brad convinces Rod's friends (Dan, Ricky and even Paddy) that Rod has betrayed them. These feelings are aggravated when Rod goes to a party with Beth and all of her girlfriends--to which Dan, Ricky and Paddy were not invited. Life in Bourke is no longer free and easy for Rod as all his friends turn away from him.

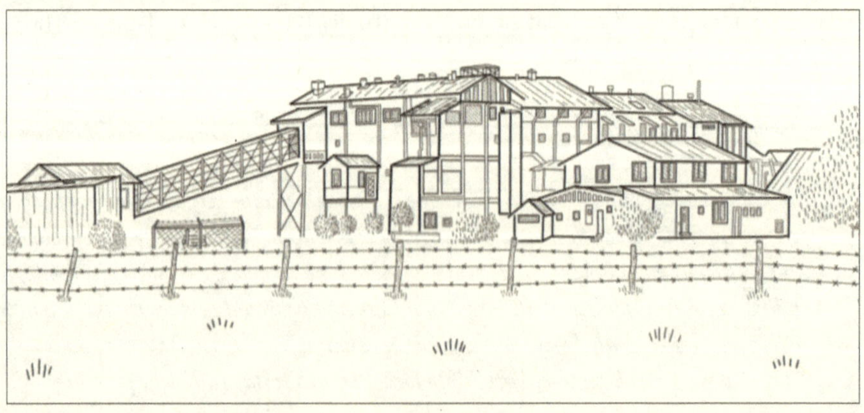

The Killing Room challenge, thrown out like a gauntlet across Rod's path, maintains the tension on the storyline and it only becomes apparent in Chapter 14 that this involves meeting Brad in the 'killing room' of the meatworks, a looming challenge to which he must rise if he is to maintain any standing in his peer group.

The bike race challenge follows the killing room incident, and then alienation from his friend group, further driving the tension forward.

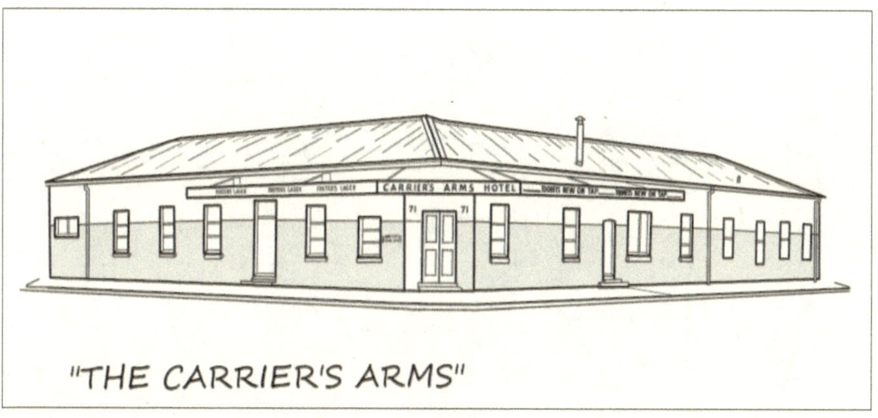

"THE CARRIER'S ARMS"

When Rod begins frequenting the Carrier's Arms, a 'black pub', and starts associating with an indigenous Australian girl, no one is pleased. His friends can't understand why he would choose these others over them, and even his cousin René, recognising Rod's naivety, is concerned for his wellbeing. In the end Rod finds himself outcast and alone and, finally, it takes Carla to explain the social norms (in words that she has never had to vocalize before) when they talk in the scene on the front porch of René and Rod's home.

> *"You've gotta understand about that, Rod. I can't just do as I like. There's a heap of unwritten rules that you can't read, being an outsider. You grow up with them here, so nobody ever has to explain them to you. They just are! Everybody living here, your friends, my friends, everyone knows about them."*

Later, Brad and his mob, are incensed by the growing relationship between their 'sheila' Carla and the outsider, Rod. Perceiving the outsider as a threat to the girl they have known all their lives, they become openly hostile and Rod must watch where he goes in town.

It seems he and Carla, in their forbidden friendship, are left standing alone facing off against the entire town. Even Rod's cousin, René, is concerned. The tension within his friend group heightens until it seems there is no solution and Rod hits rock bottom by the end of his first summer.

Rod must work increasingly harder to resolve or avoid these tensions, which carry across into his second summer when he is stationed in a field camp at Eldorado Homestead—two hours' drive from Bourke in dry conditions. Despite forming a deep bond with the desert landscape, Rod's frustrations grow and he soon feels trapped, having to rely on the project geologist for transport into Bourke on their Sundays off. Rod even hatches a complex plan to freight his motorcycle to Bourke on a goods train, but it only arrives at summer's end.

Tension peaks during the second summer when Brad appears as a station hand at Toorale and, to Rod's dismay, is assigned to work with him. Relief only comes towards the end of the novel when, together, Brad and Rod must rescue Mrs. Fenwick from the floodwaters. Finally, Rod comes to realise what he had long suspected, that tension is nothing more than misunderstanding between socio-cultural groups, that evil is non-existent, and that all humanity is indeed good and intrinsically linked to the Earth from whence it evolved.

Romance

Rod's developing romantic relationships are a beautiful second thread to the *Outback Summer* story woven delicately into the first. Tantalising opportunities are presented to him and are then taken away, through life's changing circumstances. Rod falls in love with a string of interesting girls, each becoming the object of his coming-of-age dreams.

Coincidentally, each one is progressively less like himself until finally his relationship with Carla seems doomed simply because they are from such different backgrounds—Rod being a white privileged male and Carla a black socially disadvantaged female. Rod, however, does not see these differences, refusing to accept them even as the evidence presents itself to him. Perhaps this is how we should all view life because, after all, we are one human race. On the other hand, to notice, accept and understand our differences, means we can work to rectify them and level the playing field for all.

Frustration grows here as Rod discovers he is powerless to alter the path of his own life—let alone that of others. Friends and potential romance seem to be repeatedly stolen from him by circumstance beyond his control. Suzie must return to Adelaide before he can get to know her better, Beth has already promised herself to another, despite their mutual attraction, and both Carla and he must follow different paths out of Bourke at the end of his first outback summer:
1. Suzie is of similar age to Rod, a city girl doing work experience with Adelaide Drillers, her dad's exploration company, and she is headed for university with big goals, ambitions and dreams. Similar to Rod in many ways, she would be an ideal match for him, were they not being pushed apart by life's random circumstances, and Rod is painfully aware of this fact.

> *"He pictured his and Suzie's lives; straight lines being drawn on a blank page, starting in opposite corners, coming together for the briefest of moments through a strange coincidence of events, intersecting momentarily, then moving apart, diverging on their predestined trajectory. He felt pathetic, utterly powerless to change or control the course of his own life or anyone else's for that matter. His duties and commitments, his studies, his job, his responsibilities to his parents and everyone else, sat upon him like a massive lead weight. He could feel it crushing the free spirit within him."*

2. Beth is a Bourke girl, the sister of a work mate. She goes to the local high school and hangs out with the gang at the pool most afternoons. Despite her admiration for Rod, she believes her destiny lies as a farm hand's girlfriend. She is loyal to that image and is unable to see beyond it. Despite their differences, she would be a good match for Rod, if not held back by her promise to another. She also knows Rod must leave Bourke at the end of summer, and that any long-distance relationship with him would not likely last for long.

"She was far more pragmatic than Rod. She'd hit him with the very thought he'd pushed farthest from his mind; the horrible thought he was refusing to accept. He loved Bourke, his new friends and his work, and never wanted to leave the place. He knew his seemingly endless summer would eventually draw to a close and he would be duty-bound to return to Sydney, to the family home, to his university studies."

3. Carla is also a Bourke girl and goes to the same local high school as Beth, but she is from a poorer part of town. Rod first encounters Carla when she nearly crashes her bike into him (because he is daydreaming) spilling her family's groceries onto the footpath. They connect again at a disco in the Carrier's Arms when he empties out a glass of wine she is holding;

"You don't have to do this, y' know." As hard as it was for him to do, Rod maintained full eye contact with her. "They've got no right at all to give this stuff to you, nobody's got that right. I refuse to drink it now, if anybody ever offers me some." Somehow his words had managed to come out smoothly, clearly, as he had intended.

Carla met Rod's gaze shyly. She was listening, but she didn't say anything, so Rod dared continue. He knew he didn't have much time left, maybe just a few seconds more, at best…

"You shouldn't be wasting your time here. There're so many other better things to do—to study, to learn. You're young, beautiful," Rod could feel the colour rising in his cheeks as he dared use that word; but why not use it, it didn't matter anymore, she was about to go and he'd probably never see her again. "And you've got your whole life ahead of you, y' know—a life full of interest and adventure. There's a whole world out there waiting for you, Carla. Whatever you do, don't waste it away in here."

Their friendship is sealed in the 'neutral ground' of the Bourke Olympic Pool as Rod gives her swimming lessons. Rod begins to notice their differences slowly, though initially refusing to accept them—she can't swim, she doesn't go to the pool, and doesn't even have a swimsuit. She is also an Indigenous Australian and through her, Rod learns that the town is polarised into two distinct social groups that rarely mix despite sharing the town's streets, shops and schools. Being a small town, everyone knows each other's names, life's story and gossip, despite never having exchanged a 'hello'. The two groups occupy different social spheres and venues, and interaction is frowned upon. Carla is from one of the towns most disadvantaged groups, practically penniless with an alcoholic father and a sister who is an unmarried mother. Carla's mother is a caring Madonna who we only meet very briefly in the novel, and who holds the family together on a shoestring. Thus, Carla is the opposite of Rod in every imaginable aspect, yet, as their storylines come together, their friendship becomes public.

Rod's understanding grows as far as it can, while Carla's character also develops behind the scenes at her new school in Townsville, to the point that, when they finally reunite at the end of the second summer, she has clearly become the novel's protagonist with a wisdom and understanding, bearing and confidence, well beyond her years, and beyond that of Rod. The importance of education, both formal in the nation's great educational institutions, and informal in the home or on Country, becomes apparent, and it is only through a deep understanding of both forms of learning that a diverse human race can evolve together as a whole.

It is only revealed in the final chapter of the novel that the entire story is a cherished retelling of a time past in which ordinary memories have grown into romanticized reflections of scenes from the author's own halcyon youth—the girls, the music, the weather—all basking in the golden Arcadian glow of 1970s nostalgia.

2. THEMES AND SYMBOLISM IN THE NOVEL *OUTBACK SUMMER*

Through Rod's daily interactions, the novel explores the classic icons of 1970's Australian country town life; the swimming pool, the milk bar, the open-air cinema and pubs, and revels in the uniqueness, even comical nature, of Australian slang and diction differences between city and county. He is drawn to the town's intriguing pubs—*'ornate buildings standing like beacons in the relative darkness of Bourke's quiet streets'*, each one holding its distinctly different group of patrons. A chapter is dedicated to each of Rod's curious explorations; the Royal Hotel—the travellers and stockmen's pub; the Carrier's Arms—the Aboriginal Australian's pub; and the Oxford—the meatworkers pub. Rod is surprised by how different the cultures are within each.

HOTELS OF BOURKE

"THE ROYAL"

"THE CARRIER'S ARMS"

"THE OXFORD"

Looking behind *Outback Summer*'s coming of age narrative, a literary commentary, rich in symbolism and varied themes, is brought to life through the interaction of diverse characters in a uniquely Australian landscape.

a. Indigenous-Colonial Cultural Relationships

The unspoken cultural and socioeconomic divides of the 1970s are a major theme throughout the novel and are touched upon as Rod awakens to them—each one being a learning, yet disturbing, experience as they jar his sensibilities of human equality and equal opportunity. He has to be dragged unwillingly through each and every one, especially when they become closely personal in his relationship with Carla.

A significant theme of the novel is indigenous-colonial relationships, which is hinted at even in the opening paragraph when the narrator describes the Mitchell Highway as being,

> "*designed with a ruler and the stroke of a pen to lay open great Australian interior co conquest from the east*".

It is a telling first line, as the novel's protagonist Rod Conway is barely aware of the country's 60,000-year indigenous history and has zero understanding of indigenous culture. He says to René;

> "*I didn't think there were any more of them left, René? I've never seen one before. Are there many?*"

This is, of course, due to the skewed attitude of the media, entertainment industry and educational system of the time leaving most Australians more aware of the First Nations people of North America than the customs and beliefs of their country's own indigenous inhabitants. It is little wonder then, that such a deficit of local knowledge, plus rising popularity of 'Cowboy and Indian Westerns', should leave Rod wondering

> "*if they scalped their hapless victims like the Apaches did*", and, naturally, siding with the invading colonialists "*with their gold-buttoned red jackets,*

> *black hats and rifles, firing down from their log-walled stockade upon the bloodthirsty natives threatening the settlement with their spear-throwing savagery,".*

Rod quickly beings his education when, in Chapter 2, he discovers people living in parts of town where, according to his cousin René,

> *"Nobody ever comes through these parts except to dump their rubbish".*

Rod discovers an almost-apartheid-like division in the town's drinking establishments and even amongst the otherwise-well-meaning adolescents in his friend group.

Through meeting Chief and Carla, his understanding of indigenous beliefs and practices steadily grows. Rod comes to realise that these cultural beliefs are far more spiritual, environmental and connected with Country than he could have possibly imagined, considering his background of growing up in Sydney's privileged North Shore.

Rod's awareness heightens as he negotiates new difficulties arising from his personal explorations about town. He realises that conflicts and barriers arise through little more than misunderstandings of the other perspective. He learns that all who live and work on the land become closely familiar with its ways, and develop their own particular love of, and connection with, Country. The Indigenous Elder, the Shearer, the Stockman, the Farmer and the Geologist each love the land upon which they work in their own way—the Chief in a more respectful, environmentally sensitive and traditional manner and the others perhaps in a style more akin to that of A. Banjo Paterson's 'Man from Snowy River' in which the land must be conquered, like the breaking of a wild brumby.

b. Unique aspects of Australian Mateship

The theme of mateship in an Australian cultural context is explored throughout the novel, particularly in the killing room chapter. Khara (2020) describes the often-closed culture of the abattoir based on the horrific bloody nature of the job where workers are subject to traumatic stress similar to that experienced by soldiers. The gross sight, sound and smell of mass death experienced by Meatworkers on a daily basis is incomprehensible to workers in other fields resulting in meatworkers bonding strongly as mates in their shared experience both during and outside of work. As such, the meatworks subculture is one where mates must constantly prove themselves worthy to be members of the group—to be covered in blood, offal and urine and having to constantly stare death in the face without flinching is the test. In this environment, the bonds of mateship can be tested to the point of near death in the case of a greenhorn initiate.

Rod is brought to the meatworks with the aim of subjecting him to the horrors of that place in order to humiliate and defeat him. He passes this test—just;

> *"Y' didn't get this one t' wet himself, mate," one of the workers said, turning away disappointed. Bored with the game now, the others disappeared to enjoy the remaining few moments of their smoko, leaving Rod alone in the room with Brad. He knew it was time for him to go too.".*

It is clear that each and every one of the meatworkers, and any other poor soul who strayed into their group, has undergone the same initiation—the aim being to test and humiliate as a rite of passage. Rod is even treated reasonably civilly, as far as life in the meat works goes, and allowed to return from this bloody underworld, *"to leave that dingy hell-hole of a place, never to darken its doors again; his job lay in the bright sunshine under clear blue skies"*.

Similarly, the bike race is another such test, but one Rod was not expected to pass, the humiliation of losing instead falling on Brad, whose resentment of Rod, naturally, grows.

In a short scene between Brad and his brother Dan in the backyard of their home, the only time in the novel where Rod is not present, Brad tells his brother that Rod's personal popularity represents a threat to him and his friend group,

> *"The girls are like the desert flowers after the rains, mate. He'll get in there, rooting around, like the filthy feral pig from the city he is—root 'em all up with his snout lookin' for the prettiest and scatter 'em about. Sowin' his bloody wild oats, they say. He'll piss off back to the city in a couple of months, then next season a new bloke'll come along and do the same thing—steal yer flowers or leave 'em here broken and holdin' the baby. Nah, I don't think too much of your Conman mate, I've seen it all before. That kind of bloke just spells really big trouble."*

This, in turn, causes Dan's resentment to build, thereby slowly poisoning Rod's entire friend group. There is a fine line between undying loyalty towards a good mate and the bitter edge of disappointment, even hatred, when that edge is tarnished by some perceived sleight or error of judgement. In this case, Brad fuels Rod's downfall within his circle of pool friends.

The above scene also reveals another side to Brad's character in his love and care for his younger brother, his desire that Dan finish school and his willingness to help him find a good job afterwards.

The undying mateship between Dan and Ricky is a fine example of the level of support that one mate is prepared to give to another to the bitter end in every sense. Ricky and Dan are the archetypical stereotypes of true-blue mates as idealised by Lawson and other poets.

Henry Lawson (1911) writes about mateship as a valued Australian ethic in his poetry (The Strangers' Friend), and stories (Triangles of Life and Other Stories). During his time at Toorale shearing shed, Lawson came to learn that, through thick or thin, true mates support one another—first of all in support of the establishment of just and fair working conditions (the birth of the Union movement), and then on through the severe and harsh natural disasters faced by pioneering groups. Extreme circumstances, such as floods and extreme droughts, had the ability to bring the entire community together as a single unit to fight the adversity. This concept is explored by Anita Heiss in her novel Bila Yarrudhanggalangdhuray River of Dreams, in which the able-bodied persons of the Gundagai community came together to fight the Murrumbidgee flood of 24 June 1852—Australia's deadliest, with a total of 89 lives lost. In a community normally divided along racial, or class or socio-economic status, a pair of Wiradyuri men, Yarri and Jacky Jacky, saved some 70 townsfolk from the raging floodwaters. Yarri spent three days and nights ferrying survivors to safety in his bark canoe, one by one, and today a monument to that heroism can be seen in that town. Heiss, however, does make the point, that were there a willingness to listen to Wiradyuri Elders, who understood the strength and rhythms of the river, when they offered to share their knowledge with the white settlers, then the fledgling township of Gundagai would have never been constructed on the river floodplain in the first place, as this knowledge was already there within the groups' Elders. The river simply bided its time.

The path to true mateship and fairness is a rocky one littered with obstacles of prejudice, pride and jealousy. It is a path that we, as a human race, are still walking today towards the ultimate goal of individual, national and international mateship and equality. Indeed, it is the same mateship that is displayed today with Australians as a whole coming together today to support the flood ravaged towns of, say, Lismore, or the international cooperation/mateship shown by the many nations of the world coming together to fight the threat of global warming and the ravages faced by Earth's population as a whole—in particular those vulnerable third world coastal populations lacking the economic resources to defend themselves. Perhaps Bangladesh on the Ganges-Brahmaputra-Meghna Delta, or the low-lying Pacific islands, being the best examples of nations barely eking out a daily existence and most prone to very slight changes in Earth's climate.

c. Symbolism of the Rivers versus Roads

Rivers and roads, as pathways through space and time, and as representations of the cultures that use them, are a recurrent theme throughout the novel. The tranquil waters of the Baaka (Darling River) winding a sinuous path across its fertile floodplain together with its system of anabranches, meander cutoffs, billabongs, swamps and marshes is clearly a wonderful image, romanticised by many (Pritchard 2015). The

Murray-Darling system is comparable with the world's largest river catchments, albeit it is one of the driest. When Rod sees the river for the first time, he sees it as a; "*sluggish strand of muddy brown water lying in its bare dirt channel*" and cannot imagine how it "*could've carried any kind of boat, let alone the cargo-laden paddle wheelers of old*" all the way from Adelaide at the Murray Mouth some 3,000 kilometres to Brewarrina near the Queensland border. Later when the river begins to swell with the rains, Rod prophetically dreams of the Baaka

> "*swelling into an angry torrent, overtopping its levee, and spilling into the streets of the sleeping town… beneath his room, seeping up through the cracks in the floorboards, lapping at the base o his bed. Waking next morning, he felt the slightest tinge of disappointment to find everything in his room quite dry*".

The river flooded the town in 1864, 1890 and 1921, so a levee wall was raised around the town of Bourke in 1950 to combat these regular, disruptive and costly inundations, although, as Chief points out, the river will never be contained by "*white man's levee*".

Rod's understanding deepens when he hears Chief's description of the river.

> *"Every summer the water snake awoke with the rains," the Chief continued. "It rose out of its channel and covered the river country, spreading out for miles and miles. The serpent became one with the land. It sang for the billabong birds and the eagles, and they would come. Our Baaka river called life forth from the dry parched earth."*

It began to dawn upon Rod that the Chief's River Serpent was part of a web-work of green highways crisscrossing the land, access ways for the ancient peoples through Australia's dry, parched interior lands; superhighways full of water and lined with abundant life.

By contrast with the Baaka's organic curves, Rod describes the asphalt Mitchell Highway as

> "*about 200 kilometres of dead flat straight, designed with a ruler and the stroke of a pen to lay open the great Australian interior to conquest from the east*", and later as being "*white man's black snake, running straight as an arrow… cutting an indecent swathe right through the ancient landscape*", which, instead of being a source of life is "*bare and hot and lined with road kill*".

The symbolism highlights the interaction between two diametrically opposed serpents, one of life and the other of death.

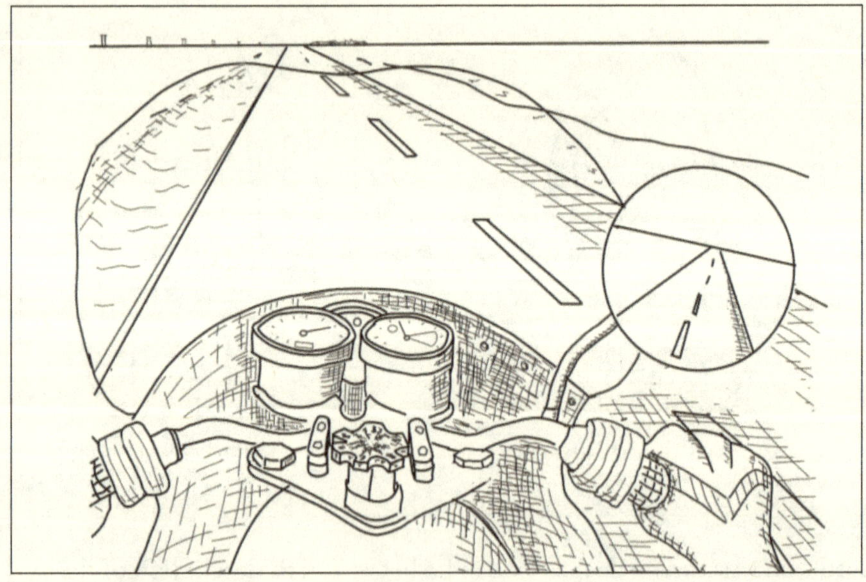

The sad image of the red-bellied black snake '*lying stinking on the side of the road'* indicate which culture's snake Rod believes currently has the upper hand in today's Australia, and furthermore Rod sees these roadways and fence lines crisscrossing the countryside as destroying the original oneness of Australia.

> *"Everybody's got their own things. They own them, like clothes, cars, boats and houses," Rod explained. "In Sydney all they think about is getting money to buy more and more things. They buy the land, cut it up into squares with fences. You can't walk anywhere anymore, only drive on roads, disconnected from the land, inside a box of glass and steel with a blaring radio. You can't sleep on the ground and watch the stars anymore, only sleep on a bed in a house. People even go inside a church to pray to God. It's like the spirit of the land's all been chopped up into tiny little wriggling pieces."*

d. Symbolism of the Swimming Pool versus the River

The local community swimming pool is an essential element of Australian culture—every country town worth its salt has one, almost every suburb of every city, and most popular beaches have a rock pool (Chen et al. 2022). Furthermore, as a nation, Australia ranks highest for the number of private pools in the backyards of suburban homes (Roy Morgan. 2024).

Australian swimming legend and Olympic champion, Dawn Fraser evokes the allure of the pool in her 1965 autobiography when she writes;

> *'My recollections of those early summers are a congested, rather confused jumble—of duckings and sunburned shoulders, of pushing other kids off the side into the water and being pushed, of jumps from the high tower, with my cheeks puffed out and my fingers firmly clamped on my nose, of hot and salty fried potatoes wrapped in newspaper, of earnest warm-night conversations under a street lamp…"*

Such sunlit, salt, vinegar and chlorine-infused memories are nostalgically familiar to most Australians of that period when summer at the beach or pool was considered an essential rite of passage. With this in mind, it is, therefore little wonder that the local 'Bourke War Memorial Pool' plays a key role in the '*Outback Summer*' story.

When Rod visits the Darling River at the invitation of Carla's brother Joey, he enters the river's world. He falls under its spell, realising it to be a beautiful place, yet, for the inexperienced, it is a treacherous place in its ever-present ability to claim a life, as happened to Carla and Joey's cousin.

> *"Sunlight danced on the rippled surface of the river—the scene before him a delicate play in brown, gold and olive tones in contrast to the vibrant grass-green and aqua hues of the open-skyed pool environment he was used to. The dusty bank below him plunged steeply into the opaque waters of the river as they swirled around fallen limbs and tree roots sticking out at grotesque angles and telling of what snags lurked dangerously below. Rod could imagine Joey's mother not being keen on the idea of her kids swimming here, worrying about the ever-present risk of another tragedy."*

During Rod's second summer based at El Dorado Homestead on the banks of the Darling, he becomes more familiar with the river, swimming in it every day after work, yet the pool remains steadfastly the central focus of his desire to return to Bourke—it is where he spent most afternoons and weekends, where he met his friends, and where he passed most of his time with Carla. Rod's halcyon memories, which have crystalised into Renaissance-themed, Arcadian poolside scenes of youthful bodies basking on verdant lawns in the golden afternoon light, are brutally crushed when he has the brief opportunity to return a little over a year later.
Rod awakens to the fact that time stands still for no one. He is forced back into reality with the sage words of Roscoe, the pool attendant, who has a more practical grasp of the situation;

> *"New year, new bunch of kids—it's always the same," he replied philosophically. "Y' might find one or two though."*

By chance Rod meets Donna at the pool, who, now married and pregnant, has clearly moved on to the next phase of her life.

The swimming pool, however, has a darker side in Australian history as a divisive symbol, a theme which is only gently touched upon in the novel:

Firstly, a fee, albeit small, is charged for entry into most municipal pools. Carla's brother Joey doesn't come to the pool because he doesn't have this fee. Instead, he prefers to swim with his friends in the river which is free, and chooses to spend the coins Rod gives him on lollies. Carla also points out the obvious to Rod—that one needs to own a swimsuit to go in the pool—when he asks her why she doesn't just use her shorts and t-shirt, she replies;

> *"No, the pool people don't like that. Clothes aren't allowed in,"*

Secondly, a sad fact is that, just a short decade earlier, Indigenous Australians were forbidden entry into community swimming pools in some municipalities, which inspired Charles Perkins and other Sydney University students to undertake a 15-day tour of regional NSW including the towns of Walgett, Moree, Grafton and Lismore. This tour, known as the Freedom Ride, was a milestone event in Australian history, pointing out to the general public the injustices faced on a daily basis by Aboriginal Australians (Curthoys 1965), and leading to the 1967 Referendum in which over 90 per cent of Australians voted to amend the Constitution (National Museum of Australia), changing it so that that Aboriginal people would be counted as part of the Australian population and acknowledged as equal citizens.

As the story unfolds, the pool recedes as a symbol while Country, and River emerge as more powerful and permanent elements, and the novel explores how different groups of people living and working on the land connect with these elements. It becomes clear that time and closeness are needed to grow an intimate relationship with, even a love of, what might initially appear to be a miserable, dry, hot, inhospitable and dangerous landscape as described by bush poet Henry Lawson who worked at Toorale as a roustabout during 1892-1893. In fact, a public war of words broke out between the well-known, socially connected A. Banjo Paterson and the oft-penniless, down-to-earth Henry Lawson when J.F. Archibald published their poetry and stories in his Bulletin newspaper airing their differing points of view (Connellan, 2013) and fanning the flames between the two rivals much to the delight of the Bulletin readership of the day (Greguric 2021). They became the two distinct and opposing voices of the land with Paterson claiming that Lawson presented an overly negative and miserable viewpoint, while Lawson claimed that Paterson was an overly idealistic, city-dwelling dreamer. Upon reflection, Lawson later changed his viewpoint, writing that what shone above all the misery was 'mateship' between the people when faced with adversity, such as the all-too-common floods and droughts.

Outback Summer joins the ranks of iconic books that fuelled Australiana cult movies surfing the 'New Wave' of Australian film and television of the 1970s and 80s (Wikipedia). Such books—including *Wake in Fright* (Cook 1961) set in the mining town of Bundanyabba (Broken Hill) and, later, *Deadly Unna?* set in a small South Australian coastal town (Gwynne, 1998)—enjoy continuing success today owing to the ongoing popularity of Australiana themes in today's international marketplace.

Outback Summer, however, leans towards Paterson's romantic viewpoint. While still exploring important issues such as interracial tension, unemployment and alcoholism from the perspective of a naive white youth, *Outback Summer* differs from the other books as its protagonist is in love with the town of Bourke and its people. In Deadly Unna? and Wake in Fright these elements are fictionalised as dark and adversarial. Author Jacqueline Kent, Cook's wife, said (Hartley, 2018),

> *"Ken had a real love/hate thing for the bush—the people he found there he felt were mean and nasty and the writing of Wake in Fright developed from that tension."*

That menace is captured so well in Ted Kotcheff's 1971 classic movie of the same name (National Film and Sound Archive of Australia), and more recently in Kitty Green's similarly-themed 2023 movie, The Royal Hotel.

e. Magical Realism

The novel makes use of magical realism to explore the relationship of Indigenous Australians, through Carla, to their landscape, particularly the river.

Rod experiences three moments of surrealistic magic in the novel, each time in the company of Carla, suggesting that Carla is somehow the conduit of that magic and that pure magic can really happen between people deeply in love with one another and in connection with the greater spiritual powers.

The first is at Polygonum Billabong when Carla invites Rod to share her profound connection to the land

> *Carla stood and gazed out over the billabong. "When you told me about how you felt about water at the swimming pool, I thought you might have the connection, Rod. I knew it. Out here you can really feel it. It's strong, really strong. Here we can share without speaking." She took his hand, instructing him. "Close your eyes, Rod, clear your thoughts and concentrate. Feel what I am feeling."*
>
> *Rod relaxed, enjoying the feel of her hand in his. He cast his mind back, imagining the scene. It was as if he were in a trance, or a dream, the edges of it surreal, blurry as Carla's memories flowed in. She stood beside him leading him, her body naked, ochre-painted; they were no longer in the present. Hand in hand, minds united as one—their blood coursing through joined veins.*

The fragility of the Murray-Darling River system, and its current abuse as a result of over-allocation of water allotments to cotton farmers, is felt physically when Rod and Carla take the river's perspective by becoming one with it;

> *"Suddenly they felt themselves being lifted up and stretched. Rod and Carla, ying and yang, boy and girl, black and white, country and city, opposites intertwined into one body, fingers and toes growing longer and thinner, and reaching far into every corner of the grand expanse of eastern Australia—northwards far into Queensland, eastwards into the Great Dividing Range and Snowy Mountains and out into the Western Desert. Their trunk powerful and strong, coursing ever southward down to the Murray mouth and out into the Great Southern Ocean. They could feel the rhythms and songs of thousands of generations past, present and future, dependent on their life-giving water."*

They literally experience what it is like to be bled dry. As a result of this visceral relationship with each other and the river, Rod and Carla are asked to take up a path in life to help the river survive as a viable ecosystem.

"They began to feel dizzy and their mouths and throat felt dry and parched. Their power was fading—their main trunk was drying out. The Murray Mouth was already dry—withering away, they could no longer spread their life-giving water over the plains."

The second instance of magical realism takes place between Rod and Carla when it draws them together during their last day at the pool. They kiss for the first time and Rod pledges his undying love.

"I love you too, Carla, I'll always love you and I'm going to wait for you, for as long as it takes."

The heavens and the stars invisible beyond the blue vault spun, weaving a silken cocoon around them, sealing them into their own sacred place on that otherwise crowded, noisy pool lawn. The river serpent, their shared spirit now, rose from the Baaka, from the earth beneath them, pushing through the grass, twining its meandering loops around Rod and Carla, around their legs. Rod could feel its raw power, surging upwards, majestically drawing their bodies closer, its coils tightening, until their lips touched, gently, tenderly, for a beautiful moment; a moment when all time stood perfectly still.

And again, in the final climactic scene of the novel

Something unbelievably powerful was rising deep within them, drawing them together, and toward one another and toward the river.

As they gazed over the river, its serpentine coils began to crystallize; its waters, firming and becoming solid. The river's shimmering surface seemed to quicken into a glistening eel-skin; it's surface no longer flat, rising towards the middle and withdrawing from the banks, exposing their feet which had been resting in its coolness. Bright flashes pulsed across its surface and deep within its translucent crystalline body, rippling like static electricity. Unable to comprehend what he was looking at, even being here with Carla too good to be true, he shook himself to ensure he wasn't dreaming. Perhaps he was fantasizing? Rod slid his hands over Carla's shoulders and back, feeling her solidness. He squeezed her tight around the waist drawing her body yet closer to his as she moaned in pleasure. She felt firm and real, alive and warm, yet, surrounding them, the stately, solid River Red Gums seemed to sway in a surreal rhythm despite the stillness of that sunny summer's afternoon.

Magical realism is an important element of the novel (especially for those who have yet not experienced it for themselves) as it brings to life the deep connection between Country and its sentient inhabitants upon whom Earth itself has bequeathed life. Carla explains to Rod this deep and complex connection in the following passage:

> *"The lights illuminate the paths those who came before and, in turn, our own. The river is showing us it is really alive; a vital piece in the jigsaw of the planet's living green cloak. It's part of the same complex web of life to which we belong. We're not separate or apart from this land, we are one with it. We sleep when it sleeps and wake when it wakes with the dawn sunlight and morning chorus. We hunt, gather and eat from its bounteous green robes. We are its extremities, its fingers. We dig into its rich earth to plant crops, and you dig even deeper to extract its golden riches which we also need in our lives."*

To which Rod replies:

> *"I believe you, beyond question of a doubt. I know it to be true and I'm gonna do everything I can too," … "I need no further proof."*

Carla's enlightened beliefs are prescient of these thoughts and ideas becoming accepted by mainstream Western science, largely through the work of James Lovelock (Gribbin 2022). Lovelock developed the Gaia concept during the 1960s, however it gained little attention until he published his first book 'Gaia' in 1979.

f. Alcohol

A series of incidents involving alcohol lead the protagonist, Rod Conway, to conclude that drinking is an agent working counter to society's best interests and serving only to destroy people's lives. This begins with Rod's memories of the downfall of Freddie the Failure during his school days:

> *"Perhaps because what he'd seen it do to his schoolmates. One mate in particular degenerated at every party, his long-time girlfriend desperately dragging his pathetic slug-like body toward the toilet for him to throw up. She was usually too late,*

> *mopping up after him. It was inevitable she'd leave him in the end, which only made matters worse, completing his downward spiral into a miserable, snivelling sad-sack. Alcohol ruled his life after that and he'd just sit crying quietly by himself in the corner. Nobody could help him after he hit rock bottom, and eventually everyone gave up trying."*

Rod's general unease with the substance being used on a daily basis grows, and even his cousin René's offer of a beer makes him feel uncomfortable.

> *He'd never been offered a beer by René before, or anyone in his family for that matter. He couldn't remember René ever drinking. Rod's mates were all into beer—well one year they weren't and the next moment everybody was into it like some kind of teenage rite of passage. He couldn't see the use himself.*

His discomfort grows when he visits Bourke's pubs and sees their powerful lure on his workmates who are more than willing to graduate from far more wholesome meeting places such as the Elysian Café, Morrall's Bakery or the swimming pool. In the Carrier's Arms and Oxford Hotel, Rod learns that alcohol is the soothing social relaxant lubricating people into sharing stories of their acts and great deeds that are nothing more than hollow dreams under the harsh spotlight of reality.

> *"…and it gradually dawned upon him that he didn't want to spend his evening, spend his whole life for that matter, sitting down listening to drinking tales or telling stories about what he was going to do with his life if he weren't just so damn busy listening to stories at the pub"*

Rod's conclusions climax when Chief's storytelling façade crumbles away revealing a broken-down old man:

> *"He's tired and sick, Rod," the lady continued quietly, eyes downcast. She seemed embarrassed by what she was telling him. "He does the odd job around the place but most of the time he's never out o' bed much before supper, y' know. Then Eddie will come by and take 'im down to the Carrier's. That's his whole life, y' know; him and his mates at the Carrier's. He's got nothing else left."*

Together, all of this galvanizes Rod into the bold act of tipping out the glass of wine Carla is holding and stating exactly how he feels

> *"You don't have to do this, y' know… They've got no right at all to give this stuff to you, nobody's got that right. I refuse to drink it now, if anybody ever offers me some."*
>
> *"You shouldn't be wasting your time here. There're so many other better things to do—to study, to learn. You're young, beautiful," Rod could feel the colour rising in his cheeks as he dared use that word; but why not use it, it didn't matter anymore, she was about to go and he'd probably never see her again. "And you've got your whole life ahead of you, y' know—a life full of interest and adventure. There's a whole world out there waiting for you, Carla. Whatever you do, don't waste it away in here." He pleaded.*

Rod's position continues to harden—perhaps the final straw being when he finds his once-enthusiastic, former workmate, Dan, drinking in an empty pub at two in the afternoon.

> *His eyes stared vacantly ahead, fixed on the rows of bottles on the shelf behind the bar, barely registering Rod's presence, as his arm automatically lifted the schooner to his lips for a sip of beer. "I'm just waiting for some work to come along."*
>
> Rod was shocked. *It seemed like he'd aged an eternity in the space of just a year; his face pale and lined; his youthful vigour and excitement for life drained away completely.*

It becomes a double shock to Rod when he learns that his former mentor, Paddy, has died, also as a result of alcohol

> *"Yeah, they say he started a fight at a party. There was a real big punch up and he got king hit square in the head. He was dead by the time the cops got there…"*

g. Education

Contrary to the deleterious effects of alcohol, Rod recognises education as tantamount to his success and so it is very clear to him that Beth, Paddy and Carla could go so much further by completing their formal education—thereby opening the door to their future.

"Knowledge is the key to the world, y' know, Carla, a skeleton key capable of unlocking any door in life you may, one day, care to enter, doors leading to anywhere, any magical place you want to go. Or perhaps think of knowledge as a powerful bulldozer under your control, its massive blade capable of smashing though any barrier, any obstacle in life, blocking the highway to your goals and dreams…"

Australian high school completion rates are lower in remote and regional areas compared to major cities, and these statistics carry through to tertiary education levels, level of income, health and wellbeing, and even voter preference (Leslie et al., 2023). Amongst indigenous populations, school attendance and completion rates are shockingly low (Fredericks et al. 2022).

Rod picks up on this subtle city-country discrepancy and it pains him to realise that his friends are unknowingly making decisions leading to loss of opportunity later in their lives. Paddy points this out with respect to his own limited employment possibilities:

"Nah mate, I reckon my life ain't been that rosy compared to yours. I never finished high school. Sometimes I wish I had've though. I'd feel a little 'shamed going back now," Paddy said, opening up to Rod, becoming more reflective. "Can you imagine it… me sittin' down there with all the girls…in a uniform," he laughed."

Rod is upbeat in his response:

"Look Paddy, go see them at the school." Rod was sure, by the way Paddy was talking, that he had the brains to do anything he wanted. "You wouldn't have to sit in class with everybody else or wear a uniform. You could do your subjects by correspondence, and when you'd finished y' could go to uni and study whatever you wanted there. It's completely free nowadays."

And Rod has similar advice for both Beth and Carla:

"You've gotta only do what makes you happy. You're way too smart. You've gotta stay in school." Rod said it with conviction, looking deep into her eyes, searching for the smallest sign that he was getting through to her. "You really mean a lot to me, Beth, even if I have to be five hundred miles away in Sydney."

> *"School's really important, Carla, especially this last year. You've gotta try and go all the time and study real hard so you do well in your Higher School Certificate exams. It's not a competition, but more like your ticket to the future! And university's free, y' know Carla; you don't have to pay a cent. If you do well, they'll even pay y' a scholarship to go anywhere in the world, to study anything you want!"*

Rod even reminds Joey that he needs to go to school and, in this instance, is pleasantly surprised by his response

> *"Okay? I'm doing better than okay—I'm doin' real good at school." He replied proudly. "I come first in class in most of my tests!"*

Rod's pedantic push for the merits of education perhaps reflects the author's own personal bias, being President of FreeSchools World Literacy-Australia, an organisation providing free education to underprivileged children, particularly girls who suffer the worst, in the poorest countries of the globe.

The lack of any educational stimulus or guidance for youth outside of school hours is also an issue raised in the novel—it is an age-old problem in many societies. Obviously, the town's youth can find wholesome entertainment as a group in activities such as playing sport or swimming in the river. However, if this is not encouraged, or made interesting, inspiring or meaningful enough and there is little else to hold their attention, such youth can quickly become bored and rudderless, entertaining themselves with the destruction of public and private property.

After spending some time with the children in the park, when it comes time for Rod to leave, they literally beg him to stay.

> *"Some of us are going to hang round a bit, maybe head over to the main street an' see what's happenin' down there. Why don't y' come with us?"*
>
> *"Sorry, there's a heap of important things I got to do tonight." Rod tried to cut their pleading short, kick starting his bike, making to leave, even feeling guilty as if he were spoiling their fun by going.*

Rod fails to pick up on the softly-spoken little girl's philosophical answer.

"Wish I had something important to do,"

Later, René does, however, put into perspective what their 'hanging around' in the main street might entail.

"The little buggers are throwing stones at their shop fronts for a joke, smashing the glass and running away. It's a game for them. Ed's had to replace two windows in the past six months, and they're not cheap, y' know. The police can't do anything about it either because they're under age. If they catch them, all they can do is to take them back home and have a word with their parents, but they're back out there again the next day doing the same thing."

A few days later, following up on Rene's comments and hoping to prove him wrong, Rod elicits more detail on what happens after dark, by suggesting that they might go home for dinner.

"Nah, we go hang around the main street with the older kids for a bit of fun. You can come along with us if you like."

"But everything's already closed now. It sounds pretty boring to me."

"I reckon it is boring," the smallest girl in the group admitted—the philosopher he remembered from last time. "But there's nothing else to do around here."

"Why don't you get a little job then, perhaps for a few hours each day after school? Earn some pocket money?"

"There aren't any jobs like that around here. Believe me, I've been lookin' everywhere and I know!" Joey answered for the group.

"Yeah, and even if there were any jobs, nobody would trust us to do 'em anyway," the little girl added.

If those who should be inspiring these children are unable to gain their trust and respect, then the problem has no resolution. Is this the job of the parents, the school, or the society as a whole?

Towards the end of the novel, the Chief has awoken to this realization and gained the trust and respect of the children and, acting as an Elder should, is truly teaching them in an open-air environment which is the best classroom. In the pub environment, Chief, dampened by alcohol, was limited in his ability to teach and inspire being divorced from practical experience in the great outdoors.

The details of how this might work in practice is not discussed, but the astute reader may peer behind the scene and question who is paying the Chief to teach and look after the children? Is that something he should be doing with his small group for the love of it, or should it be a funded Department of Education teaching position, so that every child in the school, regardless of their background, has the opportunity to engage with and learn about Country and its spiritual and ecological importance. A formal position in the Education Department would ensure that the teacher had the correct qualifications, insurances and certification to teach the children as well as the correct clearances, training and first aid certification and back up support to ensure the children's safety and security, and to supervise the activity and transport the children to where they had to go.

In the example given in the novel—transporting the kids to the Brewarrana Fish Traps was made possible courtesy of Bourke Bowling Club's bus. Done in an ad hoc way like this with borrowed equipment means that only small groups are able to sporadically enjoy this type of activity, whereas proper integration into a program with adequate government support, would ensure that a fun, practical cultural learning program would be available to every child in the state.

In the Epilogue we learn of Desert Pea Media, working with school children in remote communities to foster an interest in art, music and culture. DPM is a charitable organisation working towards an Australia where Original Nations people are respected, embraced and supported to live a life of their own design.

Another example is Scouting—a worldwide organisation established by Lord Robert Baden-Powell in 1907, to teach youth (initially boys) is also working to achieve this goal. Run by volunteers giving freely of their time for the benefit of youth, it teaches valuable life skills through games and exploring the outdoors—camping in tents, cooking their own food and learning to appreciate the natural environment.

h. The Coupon

Carla's $10 coupon opens the debate as to whether this innocuous blue slip of paper redeemable for ten dollar's value, and as *"handed out to the unemployed, Aborigines mostly, so that they can exchange them for food in the supermarket"* (as explained by Rene) is a valuable societal contrivance that ensures families always have a meal on the table, or an insulting commentary on the ability of their target audience to choose wisely.

René explains that

> *"Food vouchers can't be traded for anything else but food, and that means no booze or cigarettes. When Ed Symonds caught you with it, he wouldn't have known how many more you might've bought—perhaps cheating some desperate drunk out of them for five bucks apiece—then he'd figure there'd be some poor family out there short of money, whose kids are going hungry that week."*

Whereas Rod sees it from another point of view, and how unfair it must be on Carla who has to use them for shopping.

> *"How can you give somebody coupons, René? That's like telling them that they're totally incompetent. You're saying to them that they're not capable of being given real money."*

René only sees the need for an urgent solution to an immediate problem

> *"Look Rod, it is a bit degrading I guess, but what else can you do, if they're going to keep on spending all their money on grog down at the pub? And don't think that it's just the blacks that have that problem; there are a lot of white families in trouble with the drink as well." ... There's no easy solution, Rod."*
>
> *"No one's going to be blaming Carla. Nobody can pick and choose what family they're born into, Rod. Ed Symonds—everyone else around town—knows it's not her fault. Carla's family's problems are all to do with her father; nothing to do with her. Being an Aboriginal kid, she'd be so used to it anyway; that's just the way it is around here Rod. Carla wouldn't notice the difference half the time if she pulled a ten-dollar bank note or a ten-dollar coupon out of her pocket to pay for*

> *the food and neither would Ed Symonds," René concluded philosophically, then added softly, an afterthought. "Her father would spot the note though—in the blink of an eye."*

Neither René nor Ed Symmonds, the storekeeper, are racist, yet their attitude is the same as much of the rest of the town's populace. It simply reinforces the status quo of, *"that is just the way things are"*.

After Carla tells Rod a bit about her own difficult family life and especially her alcoholic father, in his mind he draws a line in the sand

> *He really didn't want to hear about any more differences between him and Carla. He couldn't imagine anything worse than a pig of a father like that, a real pathetic brute. Why couldn't everybody just be the same? Thoughts of his own family rose, mingling with her words; his own dad always ready to help, always around for him, for as long as he could ever recall, a powerful, solid, reassuring presence in his life. He felt sorry for Carla, really sorry that she could never experience that joy of a caring, loving father, instead of the deep brooding resentment she felt for the parasitic demon lurking in her home. Rod never wanted for anything in life; everything he needed was always there.*

The thought tore through Rod's mind in a blinding flash of realisation that afternoon as they hung around on the grassy surrounds of the Bourke Memorial Pool. A core axion, the central message of Christianity—all people equal under a common God. Why wasn't it like that then? God or no God, it doesn't matter, but it should be like that. The axiom is true, No one should be able to wield power over another. Such a message is too powerfully obvious to be stated so tactlessly within the pages of *Outback Summer*, however, the presence of the ten-dollar coupon itself is sufficient, and the questions and implications raised by Mr Symmonds about who they are for, who should be using them and who shouldn't be using them based on prejudiced observations are enough food for thought.

The movie Triangle of Sadness (2022), as a satirical black comedy, explores the elements of power struggle between classes in society and resultant controlling power imbalances which only in rare circumstances, evoked in the movie, may be overturned.

i. Captains James Cook and Arthur Phillip

The 1970's Australian educational system is shown to be inherently flawed at the primary and secondary levels through its focus on—celebration of—colonial Australian history to the extent that, even Carla, who has missed a significant amount of schooling, still reflects:

> *"I'm fed-up hearing about Captain James Cook's arrival in Australia in 1770, his heroic landing at Botany Bay, the hoisting of the flag ceremony; and the beginning of a brand-new British Colony. I don't even get to school every second day, and still I must've heard that same story at least once or twice a year for the past eleven years. It does begin to wear a little thin after a while y' know,"... "Like it's been burned into the back of my brain. But they never talk about what it was like beforehand—that's what I really wanna know about."*

While just a scientist and explorer in his own right, poor James has become a symbol in the novel of all that is wrong in the focus of Australian society and its educational system. Again, the absence of pre-colonial cultural syllabus is glaringly apparent, with the education system's focus firmly upon post-colonial development. Like Christopher Columbus in the Americas, James Cook and Arthur Phillip are a shining beacon to all that is wrong with colonial educational systems and the focus of those societies.

Obviously, the aims and goals of the education system are to fit the next generation into the transactional-based monetary and material system that forms the basis of western culture. It is not until the university level that the education system broadens sufficiently, particularly in the humanities and arts, to reflect upon and discuss its own basic orientations and shortcomings.

Rod is delighted when he discovers that Carla is academically gifted, but perplexed to learn she is falling between the cracks in the NSW Education System despite her intelligence. He urges her to complete school.

> *"School's really important, Carla, especially this last year. You've gotta try and go*

all the time and study real hard so you do well in your Higher School Certificate exams. It's not a competition, but more like your ticket to the future!"

Carla remained silent. Rod took a guess at what she was thinking, figuring she'd probably never thought about school as he did, nor the opportunities it could open up for her. How could she contemplate a rosy career when she was so busy surviving each day in hell? Finding nothing to lift her humdrum existence, she'd obviously taken what knowledge she could as it came along and left the rest drift by. Obviously, she was no show-off and never felt the urge to compete with her friends in exams, but to master concepts as alien as simultaneous equations without trying meant she was absolutely brilliant.

Taylor (2004) points out that, even today, up to 50 percent of high potential or "gifted" students leave school never having been recognised by the narrowly focused assessments favoured by educational systems the world over. The movie Good Will Hunting (1998) portrays an example of this in the story of Will Hunting, a janitor at MIT who has a gift for mathematics, but who needs help to find his direction in life.

j. Employment in Regional and Rural Australia

The subject of meaningful employment is not directly mentioned in the novel, but only implied. a question not answered in the novel is, what had happened to Dan. Why was he sitting in the pub in the middle of the day drinking, and the answer may relate directly, as it does in many cases, to the basic human need for meaningful employment to provide direction and give meaning in one's life. It enables one to afford a family and the essentials of life such as a home and a car. Dan mentions that he is out of work.

The key point here is that full-time meaningful employment, in a society structured around earning and spending, should therefore, be the right of every citizen who has no choice but to live within that societal framework, and should be appropriate to an individual's interests, educational level and skills set.

k. Skin colour

Reference and attitudes towards skin colour appear as a theme throughout. The golden glow of Carla's skin, linked with the golden glow of the rising and setting sun over the Australian landscape, is symbolic of an evolutionary link between a land and its evolved inhabitants, a link that is now known to be at least 65,000 years old (Hayes et al. 2022), sufficient time for a complete 'climax' symbiosis to develop between a land and its people. This parallels a Gaia concept (Lovelock 1972) in which everything living on the planet is an extension of Earth itself—the entire system—Earth and its thin green organic cloak being considered as a single evolving living entity.

A colonizing culture is one that has left its homeland and expanded into another land under whatever pretext. It is one that will be initially out of sorts with its new environment. In the case of the Northern European conquests, this incompatibility is symbolized by the ghostly whiteness of the colonialists' skin—indeed a highly dangerous disadvantage, apart from general discomfort, with incidence of skin cancer, including melanoma, continuing to climb in white populations around the world (Gordon et al. 2022) with Australia experiencing one of the highest rates in the world (Walker et al. 2022).

Subconsciously the colonizing culture recognises its incompatibility with the new environment and resents this weakness. This consciously manifests itself as a desire for brownness (Day et a. 2017). On one occasion at the pool, Rod even compares himself to Carla, claiming himself to be just as brown as her.

> *"See, we're the same, there's hardly any difference. I'm a little browner and you're more honey-coloured"* to which Carla replies. *"You're so funny Rod,"* ... *"Do you want to compare the colour under our bathers?"*

Both Rod and Ricky single out Donna because of her whiteness, with Rod telling Carla,

> "*Donna'd kill for a tan like that, y' know*" and Ricky calling her a "*freckled bitch*".

Prior to the Cancer Council Slip Slop Slap campaign of the 1980s (Walker et al. 2022), Australians sun worship and love of brownness was considered a rite of passage of Australian culture with the onset of the summer season, in which one was expected to burn to a lobster shade of red and peel before attaining a nice brown shade. Other cultures do not necessarily share this attitude such as the more stratified Asian or African societies in which brownness, particularly in women, is seen as a mark of having to labour outdoors, and hence whiteness of skin is a more desired trait with dangerous skin lightening products being in high demand in these societies (Pollock et al. 2021).

1. The Motorcycle Paradox

Rod's motorcycle, the 1969 Kawasaki Mach III, with its powerful but polluting two-stroke engine, is symbolic of a resource-hungry, smelly, dirty, industrialized society that pushes ahead at all costs and is capable of dominating the world simply through its flagrant exploitation of natural resources and complete disregard for the environment, minimising its costs while maximising its raw output. Countries that joined the industrial revolution of the 19th century remain world leaders today. Rod almost guiltily alludes to this after winning the race, when he reflects;

> *Look mate. It's you who's really got the better of the two bikes. She's brand new and reliable, compared to my old machine. I wouldn't do a thing to her because she's fine as is. My bike's only faster because she's lighter and she's been worked, but she's an old two stroke. She handles shockingly, and any hot day, I've literally got my hand over the clutch ready to pull her in in case the engine seizes and throws me onto the road. I reckon that's what happened to the last guy, before I got hold of her as a wreck. He's probably dead!*

The Kawasaki Mach III, also known colloquially as the 'Widow Maker' because so many riders have died riding it, is a nasty cheap dangerous machine (Ellis, 2014). Despite the bike's superior raw power, its motor consumed as much fuel as a small car and it is no longer manufactured today. The two-stroke motor is inherently more powerful than other motors of similar capacity because it has a power stroke every second stroke (in which the spark plug fires, driving the piston) whereas the four-stroke motor only has a power stroke once in every four strokes of the motor. The trade-off is that the two stroke requires oil mixed into its fuel to lubricate the motor which makes for a much more polluting exhaust. This oily, hazy blue coloured smoke was particularly noticeable in large cities like Bangkok and New Delhi where hundreds of thousands of these polluting machines were used for transport of people and goods. The air in these cities, particularly around major busy intersections where these machines gather at the front of the traffic and accelerate away when the light changes green, leaving the air practically unbreathable. Two-stroke machines are being phased out of most cities now, being unable to meet stricter emission regulations as the importance of public health and clean air is recognised.

The more refined and civilised Kawasaki 650, with its four-stroke motor and nearly ten more years of technological refinement is, indeed, a far superior machine, albeit heavier and slower when compared to the brute power of its superbike predecessor the Kawasaki Mach III.

The battle between the machines portrayed in the race scene symbolizes the current battle in society—the dominant, nasty, cheap, resource-hungry power versus the quieter calm of technological development. Who will win? And will we be able to avoid the major climate-change natural disasters now becoming commonplace?

Science, technology and the push of society as a whole are turning things around slowly, but the question for those of the new millennium is, indeed, will they be able to turn quickly enough?

m. The Epilogue

The epilogue places the novel in a historic context and shows that it is set in the past, but more than that—the author of the present day is writing about a past time, hence the story is coloured by a nostalgic element or a rose-tinted remembering of "life back then in the 1970's" The story itself does not need an epilogue, but an epilogue is needed to show how life has changed between the then and now. Half a century on, which sounds like a long time ago when put that way, things have changed considerably. We have lost the railway line and the banks are leaving town, you might protest, but other facilities have improved. National Parks have been gazetted, there is a Murray-Darling Authority, an Outback Centre, caters to growing tourist numbers, the paddle wheeler 'Jandra' plies the river once more, and significant Country has been returned to its Traditional Custodians. All of this must be stated, yet it must be kept in mind that there is always room for improvement.

People back then in the 1970s lived in an emptier world with the population being one half of what it is today, and the landscape available to be explored and exploited seemed endless—the deserts, the steppes, the tropical jungles filled with mineral wealth ready for the taking. However, despite the numerous changes since then, some things just never change.

3. CHARACTERS IN THE NOVEL 'OUTBACK SUMMER'

This section of the review explores each of the characters in *Outback Summer* and their relationship to the protagonist, Rod Conway.

René Schellekens

René is a mining company geologist, in charge of the Doradilla Prospect situated about 45 km south of Bourke. He is Rod's cousin, also the son of Dutch immigrants. René graduated with a BSc in geology from Monash University, Melbourne, and over the years, his influence has inspired Rod into a world of beautiful minerals and rocks and the promise of an exciting outdoor career in field geology. René is an enigmatic individual of few words; but he is one of the key mentor figures to Rod in the story.

Being about twelve years older than Rod, René does not socialise with him or his group at the pool. He generally stays at home doing the paperwork or socialises at the Oxley Club with locals of his own age, or older, who are influential figures in the town such as council members, doctors, storekeepers and the like—such as Ed Symonds, the manager of Permewans. As such he is far more aware of what goes on around town and its problems, including racial and social division, alcoholism and vandalism– problems turning parts of town into no-go zones. René is of a similar mindset to those he mixes with.

> *"It can get dangerous at times. I wouldn't come exploring around this neck of the woods, especially not on payday."*

As a field geologist, René has seen his fair share of life and knows how to get himself out of a difficult situation. As such, as he listens to Rod's tales over their evening meals, he can spot trouble on the horizon, well before Rod can recognise it himself.

René is not racist but he is well aware of the town's plain truths; firstly, that the Carrier's Arms, and other 'black' pubs are rough places he would never consider visiting himself; secondly that Rod should not be associating with groups of youth known to be smashing public property at night

> *"They're a bunch of trouble makers, those kids, coming into the main street, roaming around after dark. You don't want to be hanging around with them too much, Rod."*

When René meets Carla, he can see she is a well-mannered young girl, but he also knows her relationship with Rod contravenes the norms of Bourke society and so will more likely eventually lead both of them into trouble.

Furthermore, he knows Rod is only in Bourke for a few months and obliges Rod to be honest with Carla.

"Have you told Carla that you're only in Bourke for the summer?" René asked.

"Er…" it was Rod's turn to fall silent. He shuddered at the thought wondering if he could ever do it. "Well… I guess I haven't quite said anything just yet…"

"Don't you think it's only fair that you do?" René added

Rod promises René he will, and this forces him to confront the truth he has been refusing to acknowledge. He is also forced to face the fact that his holiday romance may seriously harm the reputation of Carla who has to live in the town long after he leaves.

René's own internal conflict arises as knows he is responsible to Rod's parents (his aunt and uncle) with a duty of care to look after young Rod. He is forced to step beyond his quiet introspective comfort zone in order to advise and instruct Rod. He does this quietly and gently.

Although Rod listens politely to everything René has to say, in René's eyes the things Rod does seem to go from bad to worse as summer progresses. René rarely fails in life but now he finds that he is, perhaps, failing in his duty of care to his young cousin. He eventually has to accept that Rod is an adult and has to make his own decisions in life.

Dan and Ricky

Dan and Ricky have been firm friends since primary school and are rarely seen apart in the story—so, in essence, they are almost one character and can be dealt with together.

In typical Australian style they are 'true blue dinkum mates' who would defend one another to the death. As young adults they need to establish their place in the town, their turf, their group of friends—they expect to live in and work around town for the rest of their lives, marry someone from their same socio-economic group, probably one of the girls from the pool gang, and end up in similar jobs to those of their parents and have similar life roles. Upon coming of age, they expect to progress from the pool and milk bar to drinking at the pub as part of their rite of passage, and by the end of Rod's second summer they have achieved this goal. In this sense they have a better understanding of their rites-of-passage than does Rod, who has specifically frozen the hands of time. Rod insists there is no better place to be than the Bourke Memorial Pool and that they should never go anywhere else.

> *'I gotta go to this thing tonight, but you guys have everything you need right here at the pool, out in the fresh air and sunshine... You've got the water, the high boards, shady trees to lie under and the girls t' talk to. What more do you need?"*

Dan idolises his older brother Brad, a daredevil with a reputation around town, but Brad left a hole in his younger brother's life after he started working at the abattoirs and left him for a new group of workmate friends down at the Oxford Hotel. So, after landing a job as field hand on the Doradilla project and meeting Rod, Dan ends up spending a lot more time with Rod at the pool and swaps allegiance. Dan and Ricky admire their new workmate/boss Rod, as he already has many of the things they want—a driver's licence, a fast, good-looking motorbike and popularity with the girls in their group. Most importantly, he has the friendship and respect of Paddy O'Sullivan. On top of that, they see Rod as already old enough to go to the pub, which he seems to do on a regular basis.

However, when Rod goes to the Oxford Hotel with Paddy and his older mates, and, on top of that, goes to Beth's party with all the girls without thinking to invite Dan and Ricky, they are deeply stung, seeing this as a betrayal of their mateship and Rod is unable to convince them otherwise. These events mark the beginning of a souring of their relationship with Rod—made worse when Dan's brother Brad steps back into the scene.

Brad reminds Dan and Ricky that Rod is an outsider, someone who will end up pinching all their girls, and they begin to mirror his fears, seeing Rod as a threat to their own security in the group. Finally, even Rods manhood is questioned when he fails to rise to Brad's challenge meet in the killing room at the meatworks.

They eventually become friends again, when Rod rises and conquers the challenges placed before him, and even seems to ignore the girls in their group for the company of an Indigenous girl, Carla. Dan and Rick's perceived feelings of being threatened ease and their resentment fades, although they now see Rod in a different light. He is now alien to themselves as he is breaking the town's unwritten social norms. Like René, they also warn Rod about the folly of heading down this path with Carla.

> *But, ya gotta remember, mate, Carla's not one of us, mate. Y' can't just hang round with her. She's different, y' know."*
>
> *"Look, Rick, it's like a Christmas present. Who cares about the wrapping paper? Y' don't ever bother about that, do y' mate? It's what's inside that counts."*
>
> *"Yeah, I gotta admit it to ya mate, that Carla is a real good looker, but you're only gonna wind up in a whole heap o' trouble. Her mob ain't gonna like it either when they find out you're hanging around with her. You're gonna have to watch your back from now on, mate!"*
>
> *"I'm just teachin' her how to swim, Rick. Nothin' serious. Nobody's ever taught her before, if you can believe that."*
>
> *"Yeah right, tell us another one mate!" Ricky laughed before heading back over to the group.*

Nobody, however can explain these unspoken social rules to Rod's satisfaction, and even when Beth tries to vocalise them for his benefit, it makes no sense to him, ending simply with the hollow words,

> *"I'm sorry but that's just the way it is…"*

Paddy O'Sullivan

Paddy is the son of Irish immigrants and probably about 20 years old when Rod first encounters him at the swimming pool. He is a born fighter and, like his parents before him has had to struggle for everything in life. He is white, but still not part of Bourke's well off. Tension and anger simmer just below the surface of his persona and he is never very far from erupting—as he commonly does at parties or whenever else he has been drinking. Being a few years older than the rest, and through fear of his unpredictable nature, Paddy has assumed the unspoken position of leader of the pool gang. The gang also admire and respect Paddy as he has graduated to the pub scene and, despite having a completely separate group of older workmates at the Oxford Hotel, he still chooses to hang out with the younger gang at the local pool.

Although Paddy chose not to complete high school due to the lure of a job and money, he is highly intelligent and recognises the pool as a nicer place to hang out, than the pub. Whereas everyone else accepts their station in life without thought or question, Paddy is fully cognizant of why things are the way they are in town and the factors keeping everybody in their set place in the social and economic hierarchy. He explains this to Rod on the night of the party.

> *"Look mate, you're not stupid by a long shot, but you haven't lived in town long enough. You're not seeing the full picture. It's a small town and you can't do a thing without everyone talkin' about it. Everybody knows everybody's business. The only jobs are at the meatworks murdering bloody cows or cooking y'self to death all day out in the cotton fields. It's back breakin' work, and y' never know what's gonna happen day to day'. Y' just have to keep fronting up every morning and see if they'll pick y' out of the line-up. If not y' just go home, sit around all day waiting, an' then go try again next morning—one boss, another boss, old boss, new boss, it's all the same thing."*

The tension exists in his character because, although he can understand all this, he is powerless to change his own position or move beyond the limited opportunities open to him.

When Paddy first sees Rod's determined but failed attempt to dominate the high board at the pool, he recognises something of himself in Rod's character and takes him under his wing. Paddy's acceptance of Rod, and the fact that Rod is an out-of-towner, are both key to his smooth entry into the gang.

Despite Paddy's acceptance of Rod and their growing friendship, he continues to test Rod, subjecting him to various tricky social or physical situations and observing his reactions—for example how will Rod react to his friends at the Oxford, or how will he react to Brad's killing room challenge, or how he will handle the motorcycle race.

Because Paddy works at the abattoirs with Brad he is somewhat influenced by Brad's continual rhetoric and also sees Brad's killing room challenge as a test that Rod must pass – just another one of life's challenges which the likes of Brad and Paddy deal with all the time—a competition, just as Dan and Rick compete with one another and Rod at work. Paddy's respect for Rod continues to grow as he rises to each test, although Rod does not recognise this fact at first—he feels humiliated. For example, after leaving Paddy and his mates at the Oxford Hotel, he shouts:

> *"The bastards, they can all go and get stuffed."*

And he reflects on the meatworks visit:

> *The day had wounded him deeply. Maybe it was all part of the give and take of life out here, walking the knife-edge line between bully and victim, nevertheless he felt isolated and betrayed. He'd handled the teasing and bullying—that had hurt—but he was disappointed his mate Paddy had turned on him again—that probably hurt him more than anything else. He felt angry too.*

Towards the end of the novel Rod learns that Paddy, despite his perceptivity and intelligence, was never able to overcome or outgrow his perceived station in Life. Rod is broken when he learns that Paddy's life has been cut tragically short:

> *Dan fell silent and automatically took another sip from his schooner. His tongue swept the froth from his upper lip. "They say he's dead, mate."*
>
> *"Dead!" he echoed. "What? Paddy?" Rod was lost for more words. Despite the oppressive heat of the summer afternoon, a sudden tremor shook his body chilling him to the bone.*
>
> *"Yeah, they say he started a fight at a party. There was a real big punch up and he got king hit square in the head. He was dead by the time the cops got there…"*
>
> *Rod couldn't hear Dan any more, his lips moving soundlessly; all of his senses had all of a sudden switched off, fused like a burnt-out light bulb. Paddy was dead, gone for ever; his short promising life ended in a moment of blind stupidity, in a stupid, bloody useless fight. That was the final straw! Rod thought at least Paddy would've found a way out of all this. What in the hell was happening around here?*
>
> *Rod felt the walls of the Central Australian closing in around him, folding over him, smothering him. What he'd hoped wouldn't happen to his mates this time round had happened. He'd tried to warn them. The very society they'd all been born into, and briefly had the opportunities of youth and vitality to change, was now moulding them back into its own—its long elastic tentacles wrapping around them, conforming them into the great Australian stereotype, this generation, his generation, just as it had done for generations before. Rod felt sick to the stomach, like he was about to throw up. He knew he had to get out of there fast, out of that stale pub, out into the fresh air. There was nothing more to say to Dan, or any of the others for that matter. There was nothing left but a whole lot of talking all*

about nothing—a whole lot of hot air, broken promises and smashed dreams.

Robert Coenraads states,

> *"It was hard for me as author to end the life of such a noble and quintessentially Australian character so heartbreakingly, but it is an unpleasant truth of our society that must be personally and deeply acknowledged. It was happening then and continues to happen today—day after day—Australian lives with so much potential are cut short due to alcohol—and this fact cannot be swept under the carpet, or framed into a miraculous happy ending."*

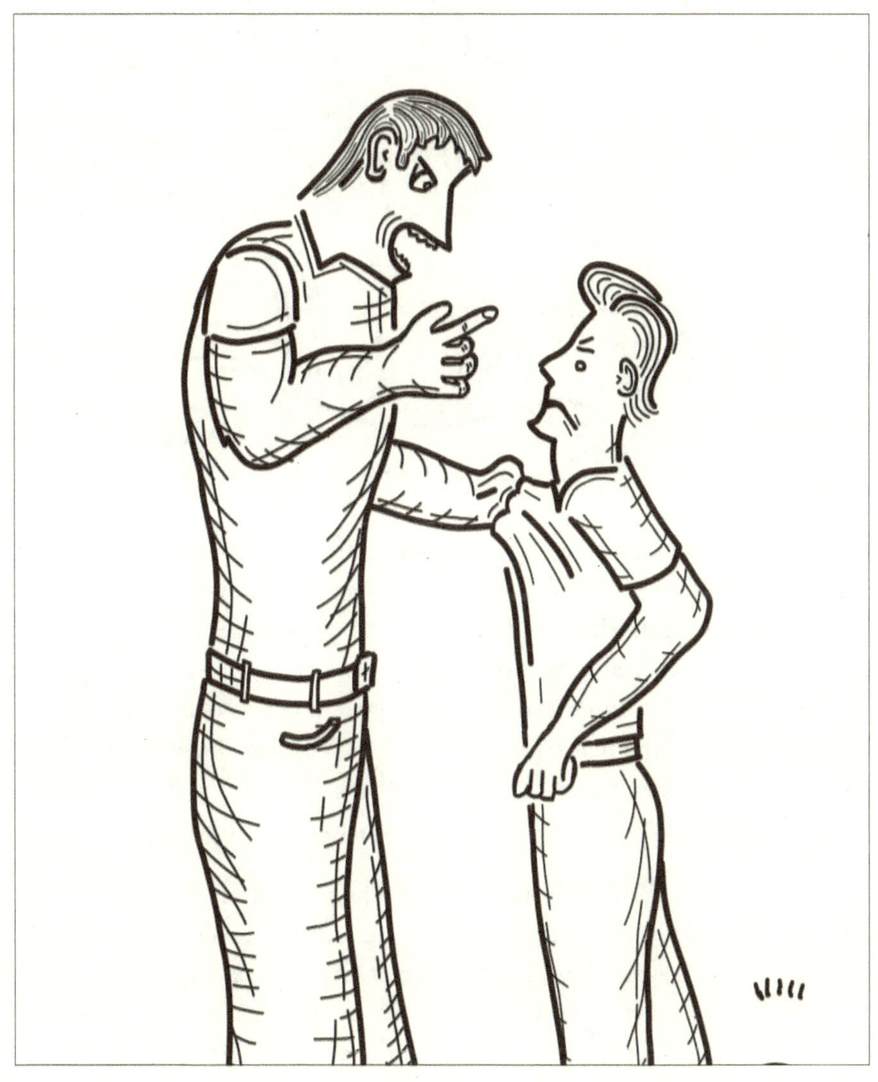

Chief

Chief is an enigmatic character—we learn nothing about his present situation nor of his past—he just is, and always has been! Rod meets Chief in the Carrier's Arms Hotel and comes to recognise Chief's deep spiritual link to Country, as well as acknowledge his own personal connectedness to the land through his work, and his yearning for an even-deeper state of connection, which he realizes most people, particularly those from the city, lack—or simply have never had the opportunity to develop in their busy modern lives. Chief is symbol of the gateway to that connection.

Such is the strength of the bond between Chief and Rod, that Rod imagines him as his own father, and pictures a life together with him in the deep past—that mysterious Arcadian dreamtime before European colonization, with Chief teaching him, passing on to him all of his traditional skills and experiences attained though a life living on, and spiritually linked to, the land.

> *Rod wondered how it would be to have Chief for a father—a wellspring of sacred knowledge lost to the modern world. During those evenings at the Carrier's, Rod felt like a son, privileged to gain a lifetime's knowledge. Drinking in Chief's words, his desire burned to become one of the nomadic folk; a tracker living each day moment by moment, reading the land. Rod's imagination transported him to those early times, naked and brown, hunting and gathering beneath the burning desert sun. He walked proudly alongside Chief…*

After visiting Chief's home for a long-awaited day on the Country of Chief's stories, Rod awakens to the fact that Chief no longer exists in the present, with his nostalgic stories of a past long lost and talking hollow words of future hope, while allowing his present, his life's vigour and the precious time when he could make a real difference, to simply rot away, to slip from his failing grasp.

Rod learns the truth from Chief's wife.

> *"He's tired and sick, Rod," the lady continued quietly, eyes downcast. She seemed embarrassed by what she was telling him. "He does the odd job around the place but most of the time he's never out o' bed much before supper, y' know. Then Eddie will come by and take 'im down to the Carrier's. That's his whole life, y' know; him and his mates at the Carrier's. He's got nothing else left."*

Rod promises her that he won't abandon Chief, but realizes that he must never chart the course of his own life down such a meaningless path—a path he realises that most people are already at risk of following—Paddy, Dan, Rick and the pool gang, or even his own mates in Sydney, like Freddie the Failure. Rod's hatred for the debilitating effects of alcohol on functioning society, and its destruction of decent hardworking lives, grows into a deeper resentment, almost a crusade, culminating in his bold emptying of a glass of wine Carla is holding into the trough.

Chiefs character turns full circle, reaching rock bottom, when Rod learns that he is Carla's father. Yet still there is hope:

> *"I know how much you admire Chief, Rod," Carla started, then paused a moment, her eyes downcast. "So, I never told you this before," she took his hand*

again, grasping it tightly, her voice subdued. "But… y' gotta know the truth now…. Chief's my father… I'm sorry Rod; I didn't want to tell you that, but there's no other way."

Rod was stunned, completely lost for words while he took in all what Carla was saying; his mind yanked roughly, like an electrical cord from its socket, disconnecting from the spiritual power of the billabong, as negative energy flowed in its place. He reflected on that vile, repugnant image he'd formed in his mind of Carla's negligent bastard of a father from all she'd told him, and now in contrast to that, all he knew about the Chief, his wonderfully gentle, kind and wise friend and mentor; a father figure to whom he felt such a close bond, like they had known one another all their lives. It couldn't be possible that they were one and the same. How could the noble Chief not be capable of being a real father to someone as special as Carla; nor care for a real family? Rod had no reply for Carla. He remembered when he'd tried to visit Chief's house—Carla's home, recalling what the old lady—Carla's mum—had told him about the Chief. Perhaps it was all starting to make sense now.

Carla concludes:

"I never wanted to spoil your feelings for him or ruin your dreams to share his world. I've wished my whole life he'd become the person you thought he was."

Through the spiritual call of his Country and the deep love of his family, Chief is granted that rare opportunity to reconnect, and recognise the dangers of the path he has been following—the vortex into which he has been sinking—and that his life was close to ending.

When Rod meets Chief again, on the banks of the Darling River at North Bourke, towards the end of the novel, he is a new and rejuvenated man.

Rod looked up and waved at the white-haired man sitting high on the bank. He looked somehow younger, prouder.

"Why don't you come up here and sit for a while, son." He called from his vantage point. "Once you've had the chance to cool off a bit with the kids."

And later, he explains to Rod how he is now more than just a storyteller, but a real leader and Elder to the up-and-coming generations.

"I spend a lot of time with the young ones these days, watchin' over them, letting them explore around the place. Sometimes they ask me about life in the olden days and I teach 'em things; 'bout the way we used to fish, trap and hunt. Next week I'm taking 'em all up to Bree, t' look at our old stone fish traps. The Bowling Club's gonna lend us their minibus for the day." He paused, thoughtfully stroking his white beard. "These kids're what Australia's future is all about y' know."

"And how's Carla doing?" Rod asked. "Joey said she's at Townsville? Y' must be proud of her, Chief?"

"Yeah, real proud I am." The Chief's face brightened, smiling. "She's my shining star, Rod." He looked at Rod and his face became serious again. "I'll never be able t' thank you and her enough for what y' done in bringin' me out to Polygonum Swamp that evening. A real wakeup call it was. My spirit's alive and free again. It was never about the river being trapped by the white man's levee. It was all about my own spirit, old and tired, trapped within the thick stone walls of the Carrier's Arms all those years. It would have been broken and busted, and I would've died last year if Carla and you hadn't come along, Rod. I'm tryin' t' help Eddie, Sammy an' the others now, but it ain't easy."

Brad (Dark Rider)

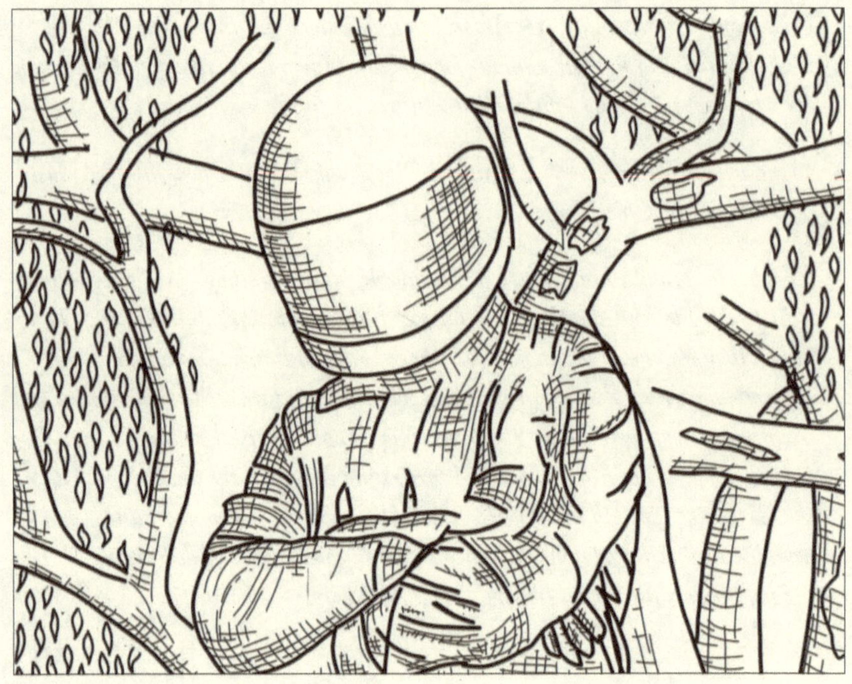

Brad is Rod's adversary throughout the novel and, as the 'Dark Rider', is the first character Rod encounters in a 'road rage' incident along the Mitchell Highway on the way to Bourke. He is Dan's elder brother, perhaps 19 or 20 years old, and works at the local abattoirs. The age difference between him and Dan means that he doesn't socialise with Dan's gang at the pool, a scene now below his age and status. He has moved on to a different group of friends that hang out at the Oxford. Although this has hurt his brother, it only serves to drive Dan onwards—one day he too will be able to go to the pub with his mates.

Brad is a taciturn character, sparing with his words, expressing himself through symbols such as his job, his motorcycle, black leathers and helmet much in the same way a peacock expresses itself through its tail.

Although Brad only hears about Rod second hand from Dan and from Paddy, tension arises because he feels threatened by Rod's presence in town. Brad senses that his brother, and even Paddy, are swapping allegiances, forcing him to share his family and friends, even Carla, with this new comer to town, and he becomes even more resentful.

By the time Brad finally meets him, the night Paddy invites Rod to the Oxford, Brad is already locked in his dark world of resentment and there is no meaningful interaction. Brad remains on the edge of the group for the entire evening, speaking only to challenge Rod to meet him on his own grounds, in the killing room at the abattoirs—a challenge Rod initially rejects until he realises that he has no other choice but to accept.

Brad's resentment lessens momentarily when Rod meets his challenge and they talk privately for a few moments afterwards, but returns following his humiliating loss in the motorcycle race with Rod.

Brad's childhood was similar to that of Carla's. He has known her since childhood, both having grown up in Bourke. Roaming the bush as a child, he has developed an impressive practical knowledge of local bushcraft, including skills such as emu egg carving. With the freedom of a new motorcycle, Brad has recently begun travelling further afield.

Brad and Carla, and the rest of their gang had always hung around together and a taste of this life is reflected in the scenes in which Rod mingles with Carla's younger brother Joey and his friends in the park and at the river. As she matured, Carla had more recently begun distancing herself from the group. Brad couldn't figure out why, and he was hurt by it. Carla never said anything concrete to him and it was always one excuse after another. She reveals the reasons, but only in her thoughts, as she sits with Rod at Wonderland open air theatre:

> *Nowadays, sometimes, out of the corner of her eye, she'd catch the older boys looking at her in a funny way. Then they'd go all dark and moody, showing off and smashing things—and they were always trying to get her off by herself somewhere. Hanging out with the gang wasn't light and fun anymore.*

When Brad learns that Carla is spending time with a stranger, he feels deeply hurt and rejected, and that pain grows into jealous anger. After Carla leaves town with her aunt Maisy, Brad interprets this as happening because all her childhood friends are no longer good enough for her. His dark feelings of rejection and inadequacy continue to grow.

Brad returns to the story during the second Summer when he comes to work at Toorale Station as a jackeroo. No one else knows of their history and when Brad is introduced to Rod it reopens deep wounds. Brad can't get over his distrust and dislike for the outsider whom he still sees as a threat. Their relationship worsens with Rod's failure to respect the significance of indigenous stone artifacts he wants to collect/steal from Mt. Talowla, an important feature in the landscape lying on an ancient song-line route with numerous indigenous campsites around its flanks. Brad drives off leaving him stranded in the bush overnight.

> *"Just leave 'em alone'" Brad repeated emphatically. "It's stealing from the dead. Can ya go to the cemetery and pinch a bunch of the headstones just because you like the looks of 'em? Hurry up and empty them out. It's getting dark and I'm going."*
>
> *It was the most words he'd ever heard Brad string together, yet still Rod persisted.*
>
> *"Don't be bloody silly. It's not stealing; headstones are different, these are just old stone tools." He went for the passenger door of the ute, but could see by the look on Brad's face that he was upset, visibly restraining his anger. Rod paused, trying to think of something else.*
>
> *"Well, you can spend all bloody night with the ancestral spirits if ya wanna think about it much longer!" Brad cut in. "Then we'll see how you feel about it in the morning."*
>
> *"Damn'" Rod swore. He figured he'd have to leave the stones behind to appease Brad. He hesitated, looking around for some landmark. Maybe next to something he could recognise, perhaps a clump of distinctive bushes. He'd just have to come back and get them some other time.*
>
> *"Hey!!" Rod spun around only to see Brad taking off towards the homestead in the Land Rover.*

Rod survives, despite almost being run over and nearly having his head shot off by Aspro and his mates who are out pig shooting on the property. Rod navigates using the 'the Southern Cross, shining like *a familiar friend in the heavens* to find his way to the road and to Toorale Homestead.

By refraining from dobbing in Brad, Rod saves his job.

> *"Geographically misplaced," Rod muttered towards the look of surprise on the sea of upturned faces seated around the kitchen table. He saw Brad there too, working away on an emu egg, quietly in the background. His anger spent on the walk, he wasn't going to start a war of words and accusations; it was close to 10:30pm and all Rod wanted to do was go to bed.*

> *"We just got back from hunting and Charlie said ya never showed up back at camp. We was just about to send out a search party for ya, mate" Aspro jeered, mocking Rod's incompetence, while Mick consoled. "I've saved ya some tea, mate. It's in the oven."*

> *"Sorry for troubling you all," Rod added, eyes downcast, but offering nothing further by way of explanation. He felt like an idiot for nearly getting killed over a bunch of old stones, and Brad was probably right—just like the bones of their creators—they weren't even his to take. He was left pondering the strangeness of that powerful urge driving him to find, collect and possess things?*

Brad and Rod are finally brought together by a savage lightning storm and flash flooding of the Warrego River. Their issues are put aside when they must work together, risking their own lives, to rescue Mrs. Fenwick stranded in her car on an island in the middle of a rapidly flooding riverbed. Later, after the floodwaters abate, Brad and Rod help Mrs. Fenwick's daughter recover the flooded vehicle.

Rod watches a relationship bloom between Brad and Mrs. Fenwick's daughter and is finally able to step beyond his self-oriented viewpoint and into Brad's shoes. He comes to understand how Brad's formative experiences in life have determined the person who he is today. Rod feels happiness for Brad despite the fact it throws into stark contrast his own desperate unhappiness in that he has been unable to find Carla.

> *Then slowly, inexplicably from nowhere, a new feeling of warmth spread through his being, a feeling of magnanimity and kindness towards his fellows. He and Brad had been arch foes for over a year, yet, in the past few days, things had changed and now he found himself wishing Brad happiness, and the same with Mrs. Fenwick's daughter, another person with a whole life story to tell; a story he hadn't even bothered to get to know.*

Suzie

Suzie is about two years younger than Rod, 17 or 18 years old, an Adelaide girl fresh out of high school and doing work experience at Doradilla Station with her dad's drilling company. She is not new to the working game having spent many a school vacation outdoors with her father in the great Australian countryside. She is tough, hardworking and intelligent, and headed for university with big goals, ambitions and dreams. She recognises similar traits in Rod, who is following the same trajectory but about two years ahead of her. As they have the brief opportunity to get to know one another at the dam, Suzie senses that Rod would be an ideal match for her, and begins to experience feelings of love for him. Two years, however, is big age difference at this rapidly unfolding stage of life, and Suzie's feelings for Rod are only short-lived as they can in no way compete with her big wide-open plans for the future. How could she even think of tying herself down to someone, let alone a life together, for any more than a brief nostalgic moment as they imagine a simple house in the tranquillity of the Australian outback? Suzie is not at all concerned by the fact that they are to be pushed apart and onto diverging paths by life's random circumstances – he is, for her, just a brief fleeting scene, one of the many to come in the passing adventure of her young life. Although Suzie, as a young attractive woman, recognises Rod's feelings for her, she is unaware, that Rod, being older, will more keenly feel the painful sting of their lives not quite being in favourable alignment. Their paths are, at the present moment, on different courses and Suzie is a tantalising dream just outside of Rod's reach.

"My God she's so beautiful it just makes me want to curl up and die!" Rod recognised that she was withdrawing from her thoughts of him now, her big bright future looming ahead; Rod could feel it, feel himself passing into history, becoming just a pleasant little scene along her life's path; but that was a painful fact for him to accept - his quiet agonising suffering was nearly unbearable as he realised he couldn't take her in his arms – perhaps yesterday at the dam, for a fleeting moment, the time might have been right – but not now. She was retreating, turning to face her own exiting future. "Should he blurt it out now, just how much he loved her? – throw himself on his knees before her, pointless blabbering words, almost grovelling and begging words. He realised just in time how absolutely pointless it would be. He'd hold onto his dignity in her eyes and they could part as good friends, with unspoilt memory of the short but beautiful experience between them, their moment in time together.

"Goodbye Rod, Thanks for thinking of dropping by to say goodbye. I hope everything goes well with the rest of your summer.

"Yeah, likewise Suzie. I really hope you enjoy uni."

Beth

Beth is a Bourke girl, the sister of Rod's work mate Pete, and one of the gang which hangs out at the local pool and goes to the local high school. She admires what she sees in Rod, who is a few years her senior. Compared to her friends, he seems cosmopolitan and smart, especially after helping her with her maths homework, and these feelings of admiration grow the more they hang out together. Despite her feelings for Rod, she is with Steve and convinced her destiny lies as a farm hand's girlfriend. While not entirely happy with her current situation, she is loyal to the notion of first love, not prepared to break that trust and unable to see beyond it. Had she come to know Rod first, despite their differences, she would have been a good match for him if not restrained by her loyalty to another. Beth, like Suzie, needs to explore her own options and forces

Rod to accept the fact that he could only become part of her life, were he to give up his studies and alter his life drastically. Rod has no counter-argument when Beth states the obvious:

> *"Rod, you're gonna have to leave Bourke an' go back to Sydney at the end of summer, right?"*

It's a fact Rod doesn't want to face that but he must. He cannot continue pretending that it should be otherwise, that one summer will just stretch out into a lifetime.

> *"Yeah, I guess I will have to, Beth." He forced himself to say it, slowly; painfully.*

When Beth tells Rod of her relationship, he discovers that people's paths are complicated and is wise enough to realise that it would be an indulgence for him to try and interfere with this for his short-term gain. Beth respects Rod both for listening to her and respecting her decision, and they become firm friends.

Later, Beth must confront her own attitude towards Bourke's racial and social divide:

> *a completely solid yet invisible barrier running right across the manicured lawn of the Bourke Memorial Pool complex on that hot sunny afternoon, dividing it completely in two… real and impenetrable as the one dividing Germany—the one made of concrete, barbed wire and steel mesh.*

when she finally meets Carla in person, it enables her to change her perceptions:

> *"You're right, Rod. She's nice."*

Like many of her friends, despite living with this social divide on a daily basis, she hadn't ever really thought about it that much before. Likewise, her parents had never really discussed it with her, because:

> *'that's the way it is around here.'*

Donna

Donna is one of the gang that hang out at the pool along with Beth, Paddy, Dan, Rick and Rod. She is highly intelligent and an ideal sparring partner for Rod in the word games that they play. It is clear that she is attracted to Rod, but also that the attraction is not reciprocated. She is "visibly upset" by the fact that Rod has been spending so much time with Carla.

Numerous studies describe the attraction mechanisms of love--those chemical and physical triggers clearly based on biological factors attuned to select the most appropriate mate for reproduction amongst other factors, such as healthy, strong individuals capable of protecting and caring for the resultant offspring.

It is an interesting question to ask as to why Rod did not immediately become attracted to Donna above all the other girls as a potential future partner as he and Donna had many things in common including interesting conversation, sense of humour and an intellectual interest in the English language, yet Rod did not select Donna, instead favouring the other girls. No matter how much Donna may have wanted Rod's attention, it was not to be the case.

The capricious and whimsical nature of love has been the theme of many tales and epics over the centuries—its iron-willed strength tested to the extremes over years. In Homer's 8th Century BC epic, Odysseus, king of Ithaca, wanders for 10 years trying to get home after the Trojan War. Odysseus is determined to return to his wife and family despite even the sexually-charged temptations he encounters on the Island of the Sirens. What is the nature of this powerful force, which in some of the stories is distilled into magical potions created by sorcery and witchcraft—yet even these potions only temporarily impede the true and natural process of attraction between righteous, strong and handsome hero and beautiful heroine, who then go on to live happily ever after.

Love cannot be bought or sold, bartered for, influenced by witchcraft or sorcery, or argued for logically—it must be willingly given and accepted.

Although not explicitly described in the novel, one would sincerely hope that Rod's feelings of love were not influenced by something so trivial as skin colour amongst his and Donna's otherwise high and lofty compatibilities! Donna is described as having "pale freckled skin that wouldn't take a tan no matter how hard she worked on it". Further, Rod tells Carla, for want of something better to say, "Donna'd kill for a tan like that, y' know".

The reader may not have given this matter such detailed thought, although I am sure that Donna must have as she watched Rod draw closer to Carla.

Ironically, it is Ricky, who once described Donna as a "freckled bitch", who was the one that ultimately won Donna's heart.

Carla

Carla is a Bourke girl, but one from the opposite side of town to Beth. In fact, she belongs to one of Bourke's most disadvantaged groups; she is aboriginal, has an alcoholic father, a sister who is an unmarried mother and her rudderless family is practically penniless, often relying on the charity of the local store owners. In these respects, she is the complete opposite to Rod with his privileged upbringing and organised family life.

Carla first comes across Rod while shopping for the family, crashing into him while riding her pushbike on the footpath. They cross paths again at a disco night in the Carrier's Arms Hotel when she goes there to meet her sister Elsie. She is intrigued by this 'out of towner' who shows interest in her wellbeing—and who is bold enough to tell her what he thinks about alcohol. His brief words strike a chord with Carla who is only too familiar with the destruction alcohol can bring to those falling into its powerful grasp. She is not used to his open naivety and innocence of his speech. Having recently crossed the transition point between child and adult, metamorphosing into a beautiful young woman, Carla finds herself no longer the unnoticed kid free-wheeling about town on her pushbike doing as she pleases - but now constantly on the defensive against unwanted attention – particularly from her own mob of friends. Moreover, she has started distancing herself from her long-standing group of childhood friends, including Brad, for this very reason—conversations have become dark, double edged and full of hidden meaning, full of a sense of testosterone-fuelled urgency and competitive pressure to see who will be the one to possess her as a girlfriend, and she doesn't feel ready for that. Nowadays Carla often feels lonely because there is nobody left in whom she can trust or confide—even though there is little time for that with the multitude of tasks that she must perform to keep her dysfunctional family together.

Rod's strange out-of-the-blue invitation to the swimming pool comes as a complete surprise to Carla.

> *"Hey, why don't you come down to the swimming pool in the arvo? I've got a whole group of nice friends there. You can meet them all." Rod blurted on the spur of the moment—nothing to lose for trying.*
>
> *"They'd never accept me." Carla answered softly, resignedly, still looking down at her shoes.*
>
> *"Yes they would," Rod replied, puzzled by her reply, glossing over it enthusiastically. I'd be there to introduce you. Y' can sit on the grass and the water's so refreshing." Barely milliseconds remained between them now.*
>
> *"Why don't you give it a go?" Rod finished.*

Despite living in Bourke her whole life, even riding past the pool complex each day on her way to and from school, she has never actually been inside. It is not a venue where she or her friends would ever hang out and, besides, it costs money to get in. She neither owns a swimsuit nor knows how to swim.

Carla observes that the out-of towner Rod has little or no understanding of the unwritten social structure and norms of Bourke's youth. He is either completely naïve or things are completely different where he comes from—but she wouldn't know because she's never been out of Bourke. Rod is neither condescending nor predatory in his attitude to Carla but shows genuine concern for her as a person, for the situation he comes to recognise she is in.

Carla realises that Rod's invitation to learn how to swim, is a challenge to which she could rise. Perhaps an opportunity to feel normal and carefree again, if only for a carefully-selected hour or two. To do that, however, she must reorganise all her chores to make the time and, on top of that, earn the entrance fee for the pool by collecting and returning empty soft drink bottles to the bottler.

It takes her a while to open up to Rod and, in the end, it happens more by accident than design, as with him she feels normal and carefree, unjudged. He doesn't ask the usual questions and treat her in the usual way.

Carla teaches Rod more about Bourke's great divide which intrigued him since his first day—a town polarised into distinct social groups that rarely mix.

> *"There's a heap of unwritten rules that you can't read, being an outsider. You grow up with them here, so nobody ever has to explain them to you. They just are! Everybody living here, your friends my friends, everyone knows about them."*

The subjects she studies at school do not particularly inspire Carla—although she can easily handle their content, she cannot see their relevance to her daily life—for example; European discovery and development of Australia, or solving maths problems. The teachers themselves fail to recognise her talents because she skips school so often that they mistake this truancy as disrespect for the system. From Carla's perspective, school is the least of her responsibilities compared with the duties she performs around the house, which include helping her mother manage her brothers, sisters, her sister's newborn child, and looking after her alcoholic father.

When Carla meets Rod again after living a year and a half with her Aunt in Townsville she has matured into a strong and powerful woman having now completed a year of Land and Environmental Management, and

Indigenous Studies at James Cook University. Her understanding from a Traditional Custodian viewpoint now openly clashes with the European colonialist's mastery and dominance of the landscape.

Rod's profession as an exploration geologist exploiting the land puts him squarely in a conflicting situation with Carla after she causes him to reflect upon it when they are together at Mt. Talowla. In this moment, he realises that he is no better than the colonial invaders of some two centuries ago.

> *"But I don't care about culture, and never have. I've adapted as I've needed to be able to dominate and conquer my environment. I'm just one in the line of succession of conquerors, and you're going to always end up hating me for that. I don't think I think in the same way as you."*

The incident has the potential for a catastrophic breakdown of their relationship.

> *"Don't you understand Carla," the words seemed to come from nowhere, "I'm not good enough for you anymore. You've grown beyond me, just as you've moved on from your town, your school and your mates." It was the last thing he wanted to admit, but now was the time for honesty. "You'd be much better off going your own way with your new activist friends from campus. C'mon I'd better take you back home now."*

Carla saves the day appealing to the strength of their love.

> *I'm not interested in anyone else, Rod. I haven't stopped thinking about you all term… And I want to spend my life with you..."*

Their love, and the strength, vitality and enthusiasm of youth, determination and driving power, turn this into the nucleus of a driving force for growth in which both Rod and Carla vow to change their careers in directions that will serve and benefit their society as a whole.

Having matured in her attitudes under the tutelage of her aunt Maisie, Carla now teaches Rod deeper and more spiritual meaning. Although their love of the land is the same, Carla teaches about the ongoing harmony and co-operative bond in which County owns People rather than the other way around. It is a deep and lasting relationship that causes the short hard struggles of the European pioneers to pale into insignificance. It mirrors the depth of her relationship with Rod when she tells him:

> *"If you want to share my journey, Rod, you have to understand where I've come from."*

The end of Carla's essay, which she has given Rod to read, illustrates how fully she has now come to grasp the plight of her people:

> *"Since when do the victors in battle ever acknowledge the losers? Especially if they don't even realize they've been in a battle and won, or even that there are losers. The winners reply, "what battle, what victors, what losers?" And the losers who have lost so utterly and completely, they're not even acknowledged as being losers, to the point that they themselves don't even realise what they have lost. They're*

devalued to the point of personae non gratae in a Terra Nullius—nobodies in a no-man's land, simply existing day-to-day in a cycle of hopeless misery and despair. If you dwell on it, it might not make you feel so good, so perhaps it's better to put in the effort to resolve it and then move on…

People are people and we all share this Earth together—beneath our thin skin of race and nationality we're all the same."

The tables are then turned in the final two chapters of the novel, where the now-educated, wiser and more worldly Carla becomes teacher, indeed replacing Rod as protagonist, and able to help Rod grow in understanding, leading to the climax of the novel where the two come to a beautiful understanding together on an equal footing, pledging to each other their willingness to spend their lives together.

Aunt Maisy

Carla's Aunt Maisy lives on Queensland's Cairns-Townsville coastline and only comes to Bourke once a year or so to visit the family. She is independent and free of the day-to-day routine of her relatives in Bourke, hence is able to view their situation from an intimate yet external viewpoint. She is the only one in the family who has really noticed the creativity and intelligence hidden within the shy and softly-spoken character of her niece. During her visits over the years, she has come to recognise that Carla's difficult family situation is holding her back from achieving her true potential. Finally, she realises she has an important part to play in Carla's life. Although only a minor character in the story when she appears briefly at the end of Rod's first summer, she is pivotal to Carla's growth and development when she offers Carla the chance to live with her in Townsville and study – *with a room of her own with a desk and a lamp*. She drives to Bourke to pick up Carla and take her back to the coast.

> *"Supplies for the road," Aunt Maisy said cheerfully, unlocking her polished teal-glow blue Ford Falcon angle-parked in front of the milk bar. She caught sight of Rod standing next to Carla*
>
> *"Hello, you must be Rod, I've heard a lot about you," she smiled, her intelligent eyes studying him for a moment before returning to her niece. "Hop in the car now love, I want to make a bit of headway today so we won't be caught on the road after dark." She turned back to Rod, "Hooroo, and have a safe trip down to Sydney tomorrow, won't you, dear?"*

Characters like Aunt Maisy are like 'white knights in shining armour' that may chance along, perhaps only once or twice in an individual's life, and really lend them a vital helping hand in their journey. The influence she has had on Carla's character becomes apparent when Rod meets Carla again during his second summer in Bourke.

> *"You're really different now—a uni student and all. You're not the quiet shy girl anymore, the one that showed up at the pool for a swimming lesson."*
>
> *"I am woman hear me roar, Rod!" Carla replied confidently. "And there's an indigenous groundswell happening on campus, a lot of activist groups, so the likes of Captain Cook better keep well out of our way!"*
>
> *"Way to go, Carla! What's say we spend a bit of time travelling around once you're done with all your studies? I'll be done with my Honours by then…"*
>
> *"Or maybe I'll even beat you to it if they keep accelerating me," she smiled assuredly at him.*

Mick Tallon

Mick is a likeable, hard-drinking, fun-loving larrikin of a character who Rod meets by chance in the Royal Hotel. Thin, wiry and strong, and about 45 years old, he has settled into life as a drover/cook working with the group of cattlemen based at Toorale Station on the alluvial flats of the Darling River between Bourke and Louth. Mick shares a common bond with Rod, sharing the intimacy of a life on the land—their jobs are very similar in many respects both involving exploration and conquest of the land with both developing a deep bond with the land. Mick's stories kindle Rod's interest in the impressive Toorale mansion and its place in the pioneering history of the river country region, a land tamed by tough explorers and hard-working settlers.

> *As the evening wore on, Mick told stories of life on Toorale Station, firing Rod's imaginings—yarns of lonely campfires and starry desert nights; of long rides in the saddle with the stockmen, and of his mate, Charlie Bowman, the oldest stockman at close on a century in age. Mick's stories were of blood, sweat and tears; of hot hard work on the land; of red dust, blue skies, and blazing yellow sun. Rod had no idea whether Toorale was near or far, but it certainly sounded like a place he'd want to live and work.*

Rod crosses paths with Mick again during his second summer, when his work takes him onto the Toorale property. However, the homestead that Rod finally comes to see, is a mere shadow of its former self—sadly run down and termite ridden. It is only Mick's stories and the recollections of 96-year-old stockman Charlie Bowman keeping its memory alive – its grand entrance way flanked by two regal palms, colourful imported Italian stained-glass ceiling, marble fireplaces, ballroom and piano – its once-lovingly attended orchards and gardens and the cool wooden verandas where one could take refuge from the mid-day sun.

> *Toorale lay in sad disrepair; floral wall paper peeling away like old skin, plaster walls crumbling in places from their skeletal frame, verandah sagging miserably, its once-abundant gardens parched and uncared for. Only the two palms remained, standing majestically tall on either side of the homestead's ornate front entrance.*
>
> *"Why don't they fix up Toorale, Mick?" Rod asked. "She's been a good house all right, but now she's really falling apart."*
>
> *"The pastoral company was lookin' into doing 'er up at one stage," Mick replied slowly, recalling rumours that he'd heard about town. "But she was already too far gone.*

The crumbling and abandoned Toorale homestead, inhabited by an ancient and dying breed of stockmen, symbolises the fading world of the 18th and 19th century colonial pioneers. Indeed, today, Toorale's decay has been arrested, but only because the building has become a historic landmark managed by National Parks and Wildlife Service and is now part of Toorale National Park.

Charlie Bowman

At 96 years of age, Charlie was born into the rugged colonial era less than 100 years after European settlement and as such is a symbol of that culture and that iconic post-colonial Australia.

> *"Charlie was that kind of person who could also spin a great yarn. Charlie was retired nowadays, but he'd certainly experienced plenty of history, and entertained them nightly, never short of a tale of his youth in the district's early days."*

He represents ruggedness, resourcefulness, independence and mateship—indeed all that that is the Great Australian Dream (Lewis).

When Rod visits Toorale and meets Mick, Charlie, Clan and the other stockmen, their warm hospitality and storytelling encourage him to dream about the world of the pioneering settlers.

Charlie Bowman and Clan MacIntoch and Mick Tallon can be viewed as Rod's post-colonial mentors just as Chief represents Rod's pre-colonial mentor, and all of whom share a deep love of the timeless Australian landscape. Each of them, in their own way, nurture this growing love within Rod—handing it on down to him—their disciple.

Rod wants to share his dream with Carla, but his romantic images of a rugged European pioneering world unexpectedly clash with a timeless land predating by millennia the short-lived struggles of 19th Century. He is taken by surprise and his viewpoint is progressively dismantled when he brings Carla to Toorale to meet Mick, Charlie and Clan.

> *"Yeah, The Snowies, what a grand project that was; cheap, clean power and abundant water for a parched nation, the country's population swelling with immigrant workers, the largest wave since the gold rush days heading to the work camps in this land of milk and honey…"*
>
> *Rod always enjoyed the stories; his dad was one of those that walked in after the war when Australia threw open its doors. But today, with Carla here, he felt uneasy with that kind of talk. He glanced at her face, trying to gauge how she was taking to their 'pioneer' frame of mind—and winced a little every time old Charlie's talk came back around to taming the barren wasteland that was Australia, breaking in the young nation like a high-spirited brumby, harnessing its raw potential."*

Expecting to recreate the similar magic he experienced between himself and Suzie at the dam, he is forced to confront Carla's growing Indigenous identity and her differing attitudes about what Country means and the relationship and respect required from its Custodians (its human inhabitants).

Michael Leu

Michael is Rod's university classmate in Sydney and appears in the book during the second field season, the summer of 1979. By luck, they both secure jobs in the river country between Bourke and Louth, scheduled to begin soon after they complete their final-year metalliferous mining course in Tasmania.

> *Rod had become closer with Michael that year, perhaps being the only one able to understand his passion for the outback, and his growing sense of loss. Michael's*

mother had lived awhile in northern Australia, a slightly-built, single mum fighting zealously alongside the Gurindji People for their land rights, while Michael spent his childhood playing in the desert sands with the Gurindji kids.

A very charismatic character, Mike convinces Rod that they should drive up to Bourke together via Melbourne, where Rod is spending Christmas with his aunt and uncle. Michael returns to Sydney for his car but it breaks down, then, after various delays, eventually appears in his girlfriend Lorraise's car along with Lorraise.

Lorraise's presence in the El Dorado field camp causes a stir, breaking unwritten norms of camp life, and so, after only one night, she is sent away by Greg, the team leader, leaving with her car and Rod and Michael's only means of independence—and leaving Rod sorely regretful for not bringing his trusty motorcycle.

"Look, I'm sorry Michael, but, y' know, this is a working camp," Rod overheard. We can't have your girlfriend and her friends staying in the house. Can you imagine what would happen if we did? Unfortunately, those are the rules mate, so they'll have to go home today I'm afraid."

Like Rod, Michael is at home in the bush, and they spend hours chasing wild pigs, catching goannas, exploring for Aboriginal artefacts and diving in the Darling River for old bottles. Micheal has a .22 rifle and shoots rabbits. He guts them, makes a fire and roasts them on a spit;

y' gotta cook it up well y' know y' gotta watch out for mixo, most of 'em have got it nowadays.

Having been brought up in the bush with the indigenous kids on an outstation, and whose father lived in Germany during the war, Mike has seen and heard a lot of stuff. He explodes the 'noble savage' myth growing in Rod's head, reminding him that we are all human beings and that oftentimes *'humans are disgusting'* no matter where they come from.

There's no limit what one human will do to another, no matter who it is they'll come up with some reason or another to justify it. Hitler was the worst, and he was one of my dad's own people."

Mrs. Fenwick's Daughter

She is a good-looking, intelligent, practical country girl, and, in her persona, Rod recognises all of the attributes he so admired in the driller's daughter, Suzie. Mrs. Fenwick's daughter is not even given a first name, to signify Rod's lack of willingness to engage with her beyond a functional level. Despondent and broken over his inability to find Carla, Rod takes a back seat, thereby leaving the way completely open for Brad to take the lead. Mrs. Fenwick's daughter falls for the strong, silent and capable character of Brad, while Rod watches on broken, miserably contemplating life's random chances.

> *His life's path seemed to wind aimlessly in the spaces between everyone else's trajectories as if intersections were being deliberately thwarted. Frustrated and bored, he slumped down on the edge of the track. The sun beat mercilessly down on his back but he didn't even have the motivation to move himself into the nearby shade. The Bourke he once knew had changed so much, and when this field season was over he'd probably just end up going home. Mrs. Fenwick's daughter was real pretty; he should be trying to help her more too. He wasn't feeling so good…*

But at that very moment the tender scene growing between Brad and Mrs. Fenwick's daughter causes him to wake up to himself;

> *then slowly, inexplicably from nowhere, a new warm feeling spread slowly through his being, a feeling of magnanimity and kindness towards his fellows.*

The rescue and Mrs. Fenwick's daughter provides Rod with an opportunity to witness another side to Brad's personality, and the opportunity to finally form a friendship with him.

> *"Congratulations on a job well done, Brad." he said formally, at the same time extending his hand tentatively. Brad took it and they stood that day in the middle of the track under the clear outback skies, shaking hands for the first time.*

Rod truly felt joy at seeing some good fortune finally come Brad's way.

Joey

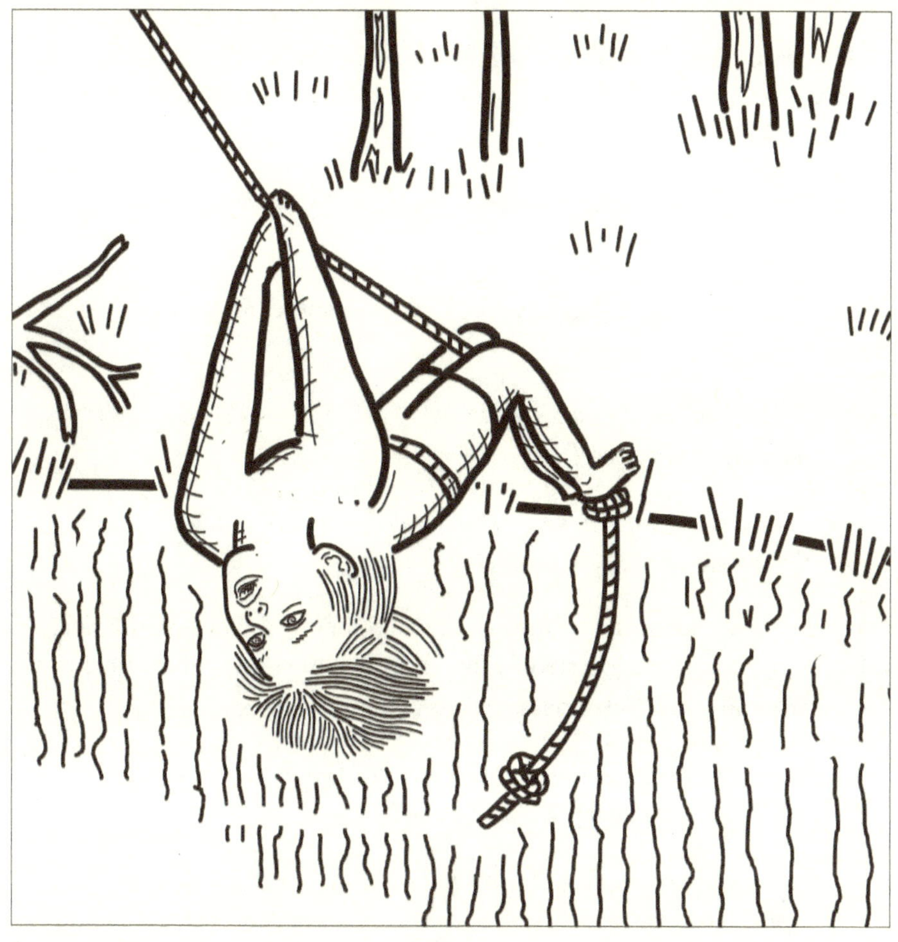

Carla's brother Joey is key to Rod's understanding of life in Bourke. His experiences with Joey and his group of friends in the park and at the river paint a near-utopian picture in which he revels, comparing the beauty of the river with his cherished pool. Joey and friends' lives provide indirect insight for Rod into how the lives of Brad and Carla and their friends would have played out in and around the town just a few short years earlier. A near-idyllic lifestyle from Rod's perspective, yet subtly fractured by ever-present danger (the river's snags and the story of a cousin's tragic drowning). At the end of the afternoon Rod makes excuses to leave:

> *"Sorry, there's a heap of important things I got to do tonight." Rod tried to cut their pleading short, kick starting his bike, making to leave, even feeling guilty as if he were spoiling their fun by going.*

However, the real problems they face are brought into focus by the little girl who echoes Rod and the truth becomes a sorry story of boredom and disadvantage.:

> *"Wish I had something important to do," a smaller girl stated matter-of-factly to no one in particular, almost philosophically.*

And again, when Rod suggests they find a job and earn some pocket money

> *"There aren't any jobs like that around here. Believe me, I've been lookin' everywhere and I know!" Joey answered for the group.*
>
> *"Yeah, and even if there were any jobs, nobody would trust us to do 'em anyway," the little girl added."*

Finally, towards the end of the novel, when they again meet in the river, Joey's journey in the footsteps of his sister becomes clear in his final conversation with Rod about going to university.

> *"I'm gonna go there too when I'm old enough," Joey said in between strokes. "Auntie Maisy's already told me I could."*
>
> *"Well good for you! As long as you're doing okay at your school work?" Rod replied, probing if Joey realized the importance of that connection. "In that case you can do anything you like."*
>
> *"Okay? I'm doing better than okay—I'm doin' real good at school." He replied proudly. "I come first in class in most of my tests!"*
>
> *Rod chuckled. "Yeah, looks like you're a clever kid. I guess it must run in the family then?"*
>
> *"Yeah, I guess so," Joey replied, thoughtful for a brief moment, as he scrambled up the far bank and grabbed the rope hanging vertically from the thick branch of the river gum. "But I'm much smarter than Carla," he called out.*

Ed Symonds

Ed Symonds is proprietor and cashier of Rite Way supermarket in Bourke's main street. In such a central position he has a wide knowledge of the comings and goings of Bourke's community—all of whom come into his store for their shopping, often on a daily basis. He is a friend of

René and they socialise often at the Oxley Club.

Carla is responsible for picking up her family's groceries each day from Rite Way, bringing them home in the basket of her bike, and so Ed Symonds also knows Carla and her family well, and is fully aware of the difficult situation in which they live. Carla is obviously embarrassed to reveal much about her family life to Rod—her unemployed alcoholic father, single-mother sister and the knife-edge of poverty in which their family live and face on a day-to-day basis. The scant detail she reveals is triggered one afternoon at the pool when Rod hands her some coins for Joey to get into the pool. Although he is daydreaming at the time, Rod learns more about Carla through Ed Symonds' short interaction with her at the checkout

> *"How's y'r mum and the rest of the kids, Carla?"*
>
> *"We're all fine thanks, Mr Symonds. And yourself and Mrs. Symonds?" Rod heard Carla answer, her words filtering through his mind, triggering lines of random thought. It's funny how you can get to know nearly everybody in a town this size. He liked how that happened, Henry Lawson's words ringing true, 'Bourke is mateship country'.*
>
> *"Here take this other bag as well, Carla. Mrs. Symonds put aside an extra bottle of milk and loaf of bread for your mum. Please give her our regards, won't you love?"*
>
> *"Thanks, Mr Symonds. Will do, I'll tell mum that. See you later." She headed out the door, a grocery bag tucked under each arm.*

Mr Symonds is a kind and compassionate character, although he then surprises Rod with his confrontational reaction to Rod being in possession of the $10 food coupon

> *"Hey mate… Where'd y' get this from?"*
>
> *"Er… I…" Rod was at a loss for words. "I gave somebody ten dollars for it." He stammered, grateful that Carla was out of hearing range.*
>
> *"Y' don't give nobody any money for these, mate! They're here for a purpose. Who'd y' get it off?"*

> *"Er…" Rod didn't know what to say. He felt pretty foolish, but he knew one thing for sure that he wasn't going to dob in Carla. What was this all about anyway he wondered. "Er… I'm not sure… I dunno who it was? Can't I use it?"*

> *"Very well then, mate." The cashier spoke in a measured tone, quietly, but obviously very angry with Rod. "You keep hold of your own money in future. I'm accepting it this time, but if I ever see you in here again with another one of these, I'm going to take it off of you, y' hear, and report you to the police?*

Later it is René who explains the reason for his friend, Mr Symonds' reaction

> *"Food vouchers can't be traded for anything else but food, and that means no booze or cigarettes. When Ed Symonds caught you with it, he wouldn't have known how many more you might've bought—perhaps cheating some desperate drunk out of them for five bucks apiece—then he'd figure there'd be some poor family out there short of money, whose kids are going hungry that week."*

Yet Mr and Mrs. Symonds very kindness and concern for the plight of Carla's family highlights the huge gulf between the different strata of Bourke society and how these prejudices are fixed in concrete—not through the fault of anyone in particular—they just are!

Conclusion

Interestingly, every character in the novel discussed here is flawed, as is every human being, all experiencing issues based on their point of view and moulded by their life's experiences. Perhaps the only perfect character is Carla, but it is clear that her less-than-favourable family circumstances are hindering her forward progress in life, limiting her, until she grasps a chance opportunity presented to her.

Unfavourable circumstances in life can either force a person to rise nobly above them, or cause them to stumble into society's negative vices which may trap, consume and ultimately destroy them completely.

4. SUMMARY

Outback Summer is a story of love between two individuals separated by a yawning cultural chasm, the story of ying versus yang, the story of city boy versus country girl, black versus white, societally advantaged versus disadvantaged. At the end of the first summer, we leave Rod and Carla, the two protagonists deeply in love after a bonding experience that surpasses anything else commonly experienced between soulmates quivering at the brink of an unknown and powerful future—tingling with sexual anticipation at the threshold of unknown adventures and wonderfully creative experiences.

The novel pushes deeply into those unknown experiences to be had in classically beautiful Arcadian landscapes. Indeed, experiences and landscapes into which each of us should be entering daily as we awake for each new day as Earth completes its twenty-four-hour rotation and the sun appears newly on the easternmost horizon, when even the birds cheer in anticipation in their morning chorus. Each and every one of us needs to attune ourselves revelling in the majesty of this experience, harnessing its euphoric positivity into our daily lives.

> *Rod drove the Land Rover back home, eastwards into the warmth of the rising sun. Somehow, the rays of golden morning light bathing the inside of the cab*

seemed to wash away his emptiness.

The hands on Rod's clock were frozen forever in the joy of the present moment.

With each day indeed being a birth and the beginning of a new adventure, running through to the end of the day when we experience a tired satisfaction at our achievements, giving them up to the greater good, to the greater Supreme Self before sinking into a deep and profound sleep. The whole process of each day is, in fact, a symbol of the cycle of our entire lives, commencing with our birth, our awakening, and growth, culminating in the very moment experienced by Rod and Carla, as described in this novel, and from there expanding into an exciting unknown full of challenges and achievements. At the end of their first summer, the deep bond and love between Rod and Calra has drawn together a yawning chasm of every imaginable difference and they now sit together on a level playing field—an aerodrome—and are ready to take off and soar into the unknown. Interwoven also into the story of the first summer of *Outback Summer* is the undeniable fact that education, of whatever sort, be it in the sciences, or arts, trades, or simply living a full life interacting with others, that this education is the key, the unique leveller and equaliser. It is the education that gives individuals and the political leadership its moral, ethical and experiential background to make decisions for the benefit of the communities which they are governing, which allow entire societies as a whole to soar into the realms of light and life,

The music chosen to accompany key moments, events and feelings experienced in the novel is largely drawn from the 1960s and 1970s to express feelings of the excitement of standing on the brink of young love, or feelings of sorrow, broken hearts and lost dreams, when the individual or situation is not quite right, songs of adventure and discovery of the unknown, songs of the jubilation, joy of homecoming and reunion, songs of yearning and imprisoned desires, songs of protest based around the Vietnam war experience when youth of the same age of the characters in this novel were forced into a meaningless war experience brought about through the whims of ideologically opposed governments.

Take a listen again to each of the songs in the playlist. Appreciate and enjoy the paragraphs in the vicinity of the reference in the novel which make tribute to the creative genius of the musicians involved in their creation and their significance to the themes presented in *Outback Summer*, to the emotions and feelings being experienced by the protagonists.

I would like to conclude with a further quote from the novel's cultural sensitivity report prepared by Jiddabal/Mamu/Yidinji Traditional Custodian, and good friend, Gerry Surha.

Iljiddimoor states:

> *The novel gives a reflection of an historical outback Australia that many of the younger generation, particularly those living in cities, have not experienced. By reading Outback Summer, I have no doubt they will benefit by getting a realistic insight into a part of that decade around which the novel revolves.*
>
> *Because of its detailed story building, I appreciated its strong characters, and the author's ability to seamlessly connect all the other stories in the novel to the lead protagonist and I highly recommend reading this novel that will end in leaving one with, only good vibrations.*
>
> *For me, this novel is a must-read for any lover of fiction/fact no matter what part of the planet you live on.*

5. BIBLIOGRAPHY

Barnes, John. 2017. The making of a legend: Henry Lawson at Bourke. The La Trobe Journal No. 99 March 2017. p. 35-49.

Chen, Chris and McDermott, Marie-Louise. 2022. Ocean Pools, 75 pools across Australia for saltwater swimmers. Thames and Hudson 272 pp.

Connellan, Ian. 2013. Timeline: The life of Henry Lawson. Australian Geographic, February 15. https://www.australiangeographic.com.au/topics/history-culture/2013/02/timeline-the-life-of-henry-lawson/

Cook, Kenneth. 1961. Wake in Fright. Michael Joseph, London /Penguin, Australia 191pp. Sold 20,000 copies in 1970's and still in print. A Ted Kotcheff film of same name was released 1971 and restored 1990.

Curthoys, Anne 1965. Freedom Ride Diaries. https://aiatsis.gov.au/collection/featured-collections/ann-curthoys-diaries.

Day et al. 2017. (Ashley K. Day, Carlene J. Wilson,Amanda D. Hutchinson and Rachel M. Roberts). Australian young adults' tanning behaviour: The role of ideal skin tone and sociocultural norms. Australian Journal of Psychology. volume 69, 2017 - Issue 2. P.86-94 | Received 23 Jun 2015, Accepted 27 Jan 2016, Published online: 20 Nov 2020. https://doi.org/10.1111/ajpy.12121

Desert Pea Media, a cross-cultural, charitable organisation working towards an Australia where Original Nations people are respected, embraced and supported to live a life of their own design. https://www.desertpeamedia.com/

Ellis, Geoffrey 2014. Kawasaki Mach III. The Quarter Mile Blaster. Old Bike Australasia, Issue No.45, pp. 38-43.

Fraser, Dawn with Harry Gordon 1965. Below the Surface Confessions of an Olympic Champion William Morrow & Co, New York. (Published in Australia under the title Gold Medal Girl, Lansdowne Press, Melbourne

Fraser, Dawn 2001. Dawn: One hell of a life. Hodder Stoughton, UK.

Fredericks, B. et al. 2022. (Bronwyn Fredericks, Katelyn Barney, Tracey Bunda, Kirsten Hausia, Anne Martin, Jacinta Elston, Brenna Bernardino, Daniel Griffiths). Building the evidence to improve completion rates for indigenous students. NCSEHE National Centre for Student Equity in Higher Education https://www.ncsehe.edu.au/publications/improve-completion-rates-indigenous-students/#:~:text=The%20national%20data%20indicates%20that,24).

Good Will Hunting. Released 12 March 1998 (Australia). Director: Gus Van Sant

Gordon L.G. et al. 2022. (Louisa G Gordon, Sophy Shih, Caroline Watts, David Goldsbury, Adèle C Green). The economics of skin cancer prevention with implications for Australia and New Zealand: where are we now? Review Public Health Res Pract. 2022 Mar 10;32(1):31502119. doi: 10.17061/phrp31502119.

Greguric, Paul J. 2021. The Man Behind the Prize: A Life of J.F. Archibald. Shawline Publishing Group. 204pp.

Gribbin, J. 2022. James E. Lovelock (1919-2022). Inventor who introduced the Gaia hypothesis to environmental science. Nature 608, 261.

Gwynne, Phillip 1998. Deadly, Unna?. Penguin 288pp. received Children's Book of the Year Award Older Readers and Victorian Premier's Prize for Young Adult Fiction in 1999. Over 180,000 copies sold. Sequel Nukkin Ya published in 2000. Released as feature film, Australian Rules, in 2002 winning an Australian Film Industry Award.

Hartley, George, 2018. Wake in Fright: You don't like the Yabba? New Diogenes Melbourne / One comment, January 4. https://newdiogenesmelbourne.wordpress.com/2018/01/04/you-dont-like-the-yabba/

Heiss, Anita 2021. Bila Yarrudhanggalangdhuray River of Dreams. Simon and Schuster. 393 pp.

Hardy, Bobbie 1976. Lament for the Barkindji. The vanished tribes of the Darling River Region. Rigby Limited, Sydney. 246 pp.

Hayes, E.H. et al 2022 (Elspeth H. Hayes, Richard Fullagar, Judith H. Field, Adelle C.F. Coster, Carney Matheson, May Nango, Djaykuk Djandjomerr, Ben Marwick, Lynley A. Wallis, Mike A. Smith & Chris Clarkson). 65,000-years of continuous grinding stone use at Madjedbebe, Northern Australia. Nature. Scientific Reports volume 12, Article number: 11747 (2022).

Khara, T. 2020. Animals suffer for meat production – and abattoir workers do too. The Conversation, published: February 5, 2020. https://theconversation.com/animals-suffer-for-meat-production-and-abattoir-workers-do-too-127506.

Lawson, Henry 1911. Mateship : a discursive yarn. Melbourne : Lothian, 1911. 77 pp. Series: Lothian's Australian miniatures

Leslie, T. et al. 2023. (Tim Leslie, Ashley Kyd, Julian Fell, Ben Spraggon and Matt Liddy). Beyond No, here's what we know about the Voice results. ABC Story Lab, 15 Oct 2023.

Lewis, Jon. Charles William Bowman Drover—Drover, a true account of the drovin' life from the Back of Bourke. Australian Geographic.

Lovelock. J.E. (1979). "Gaia: A New Look at Life on Earth. Oxford University Press. ISBN 978019217665-3.

National Museum of Australia. Australia's Defining Moments Digital Classroom. https://digital-classroom.nma.gov.au/defining-moments/indigenous-referendum

National Film and Sound Archive of Australia. Wake in Fright NFSA Restored and Re-released in 2009. https://www.nfsa.gov.au/collection/curated/wake-fright-classic-australian-film-restored-nfsa

Ogilvie, W. H. (1896) 'Back O' Bourke. Poem published in William Henry Ogilvie (1869-1963) under the pen-name of Glenrowan in the Baards of the Backblocks section of The Bulletin (Sydney, New South Wales, Australia) of Saturday 15th February 1896.

Pollock et al. 2020. (Samara Pollock, Susan Taylor, Oyetewa Oyerinde, Sabrina Nurmohamed, Ncoza Dlova, Rashmi Sarkar, Hassan Galadari, Mônica Manela-Azulay, Hae Shin Chung, Evangeline Handog, and A. Shadi Kourosh). The dark side of skin lightening: An international collaboration and review of a public health issue affecting dermatology. International Journal of Women's Dermatology 2021 Mar; 7(2): 158–164. Published online 2020 Sep 17. doi: 10.1016/j.ijwd.2020.09.006

Pritchard, Tony 2015. Drifting Down the Darling: Birdwatching and seeking wisdom in a small boat. MoshPit Publishing.

Rix, Ethan. 2024. Melanoma specialists and Australians of the Year warn nation's tanning culture is 'killing us'. ABC News Fri 26 Jan 2024.

Rommelaere, Vincent. 2021. Rock Pools of Sydney. Unseen Australia. 204 pp.

Roy Morgan Research. 2023. One-in-seven Australians (3.1 million) live in a house with a swimming pool or spa. August 15, 2023

Taylor, Catherine. 2024. Gifted and Ignored: The smart kids who can't afford to succeed. Illustrations by Gabrielle Flood and Lindsay Dunbar. ABC's Long Read. ABC News Story Lab.

Triangle of Sadness. Released 13 September 2022 (Denmark). Writer and Director: Ruben Östlund.

Walker H. et al. 2022. (Heather Walker, Clover Maitland, Tamara Tabbakh, Paige Preston, Melanie Wakefield, Craig Sinclair). Forty years of Slip! Slop! Slap! A call to action on skin cancer prevention for Australia. Review Public Health Res Pract. 2022 Mar 10;32(1):31452117. doi: 10.17061/phrp31452117.

Wikipedia. Australian New Wave, Australian Film Revival, Australian Film Renaissance—era of resurgence in worldwide popularity of Australian cinema. https://en.wikipedia.org/wiki/Australian_New_Wave

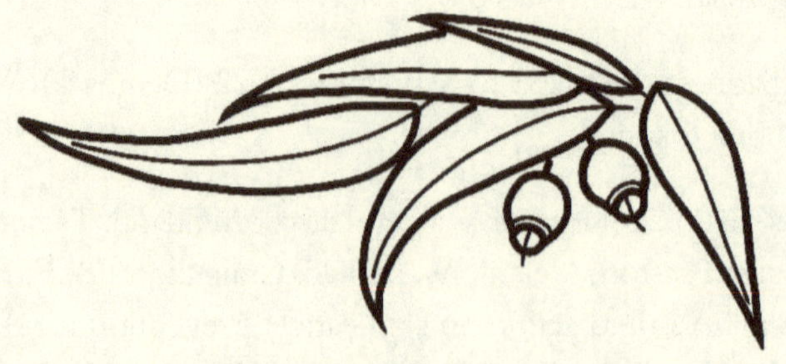

6. ABOUT THE AUTHOR

Dr Robert R. Coenraads is an artist, explorer and educator who travels the world in search of treasures such as exotic minerals, gemstones and unique cultural experiences which form the basis for his writing.

As President of FreeSchools World Literacy Australia, Dr Coenraads believes strongly in the value of education in today's society. Education betters the quality of life of individuals, lifting families, villages and entire countries out of poverty. It gives meaning, hope and purpose to those fortunate enough to receive it, bringing harmony between the diverse peoples of our planet and greater understanding of and respect for diversity and traditional cultural values and an appreciation for the pillars of Truth, Beauty and Goodness in a philosophic context/perspective as goals of individual attainment. These pillars are a means of attaining/cultivating global harmony between the diverse peoples of the planet and ultimately world peace.

Under the Lens, Literary Analysis of the Novel Outback Summer is a response to questions I have received from readers about the symbolism and themes in "*Outback Summer*" and their significance. At nearly a third of the size of the original novel, this 27,000-word book addresses those questions, while at the same time embodying my enjoyment of critical analytical studies and desire to share societally-motivated thoughts.

Even if you might not be interested in literary analysis and societal criticism, perhaps you might simply enjoy this essay as a deeper exploration of the characters from the original novel with whom you've become familiar and grown to love.

www.ingramcontent.com/pod-product-compliance
Lightning Source LLC
LaVergne TN
LVHW050934080826
845145LV00004B/1260

* 9 7 8 1 9 2 3 3 3 0 0 6 1 *